Introduction

T0243467

The Boeing Model 464 B-52 Stratofortress, later known as the 'BUFF', was the last of the legendary Seattle company's famous Fortress series of aircraft. First taking to the skies on 15 April 1952, the B-52 was almost as big as Convair's B-36, the largest serial-produced piston aircraft ever built. With its Boeing stable mates, the B-47 and the B-50, the B-52 was designed to meet the United States Air Force (USAF) Strategic Air Command's (SAC) ever-changing needs in the nuclear age.

Created over a weekend in a hotel suite in Ohio, the B-52 would give the post-war Strategic Air Command, led by General Curtis LeMay, an additional nuclear-capable edge. The B-52 would become the ultimate expression of the Cold War's Very Heavy Bomber design. As with previous Boeing designs, LeMay would be influential in the B-52s. Unlike the B-29 saga, Boeing could hit the ground running after receiving the Air Materiel Command's (AMC) specifications. Gathering some of their finest and most experienced engineers, Boeing delivered a sleek, high-wing bomber capable of carrying over 10,000lbs (4,500kg) of stores, including special weapons (nuclear). The B-52 would also have a range of 6,909mi (11,125km). Its key identifying feature would become its ubiquitous four twin-engine power pods,

The B-17, B-29 and B-52; The Boeing 'Fortress family gathered together in flight and representing two decades of Boeing innovation.

Sporting its characteristic forward fuselage pre-pressurization wrinkles, this B-52G is prepared for its next mission in support of Operation Desert Storm. (The US National Archives)

A fine air-to-air photographic study of a Boeing RB-47E. Even from this simple image the B-52's lineage is clear. (US Government)

a development of lessons learned from the B-47.

By the time the B-52 entered serial production and service with the USAF, the mission and doctrine of the SAC had been refined by LeMay and his team. As a result, the B-52 became an integral part of the United States' nuclear deterrent. From 1960 to 1968, the nuclear-armed B-52 maintained a permanent aerial presence over North America and the Mediterranean. Then, with the perfection of missile technology and its entry into service as land- and sea-launched Intercontinental Ballistic Missiles (ICBM), the nuclear-armed B-52 deterrence became redundant.

The following decades saw the B-52 develop into a strategic and tactical airborne platform capable of delivering evermore deadly attacks against targets in various environments, from jungle to arid mountains. The B-52 had become the universal tool for commanders on the ground and a symbol of American military power, capable of striking a target anywhere in the world.

The twenty-first century has seen the B-52 develop further. Boeing's rugged design can now carry an astonishing 70,000lbs (31,500kg) bomb load and fly an impressive 8,800 miles (14,200km). Despite the possible development of a four-engine conversion, both Boeing and the USAF were convinced the current engine arrangement was, in the long run, better for the B-52. Allied to upgrades in avionics,

A combat crew races to its B-52. At one point fifty per cent of the SAC bomber force was on continuous ground alert, ready to fly and engage a target within the warning time provided by the ballistic missile early warning system. Note the AGM-28 suspended from its wing pylon. (US Air Force photo)

A B-52H taking on fuel from a Boeing KC-135 flown by the 916th Air Refueling Wing of the Air Reserve Component (ARC). (Robert Sullivan)

the B-52 is destined to become one of the first military aircraft to reach the milestone of a century of service.

Such is the potency that the USAF and Boeing have developed an aeroplane of such importance that it now seems impossible to discuss conventional air power without including the B-52. This Flight Craft title offers the modeller an exciting selection of related information through photographs, illustrations, and excellent showcase examples to help readers build their versions of this legendary military aeroplane.

Eldership of the 320th Bombardment Wing, pictured at Guam during Exercise Giant Warrior 1989, was the oldest B-52G when she was retired in July 1989. (Technical Sergeant Lee Schading, USAF)

A B-52H of the 2nd Bomb Wing static display with weapons, at Barksdale Air Force Base, Louisiana, with examples of all the weapons it's capable of carrying in 2006. (Technical Sergeant Robert Horstman, USAF)

Design & Development

In 1947 the latest Boeing, the B-50, was at the cutting edge of heavy-bomber design. This is an early B-50A that has been converted to WB-50 weather reconnaissance standard. (NARA)

An airman stands by the Convair B-36 main landing gear. The B-36 was an enormous aircraft, but its size was one of its many weaknesses. (NARA)

In 1946, while the world was slowly recovering from the bloodiest war in history and adjusting to the new atomic age, Boeing was already preparing the next generation of aircraft. These futuristic aircraft would be powered by the latest marvel of the period: the turbojet, an engine the military was eager to utilize to gain an edge over the slowly emerging threat of Soviet communism. Boeing was on the verge of conducting the first flight of their six-engine Model 450, which would later become the B-47 Stratojet. Within just four years of its introduction into the USAF service, the B-52 would join the ranks of SAC's flight lines.

The development of the B-47 was partly driven by the realization that the propeller-driven bomber was nearing the end of its usefulness. There was also a desire to harness and develop the technology and engineering required for jet flight to create a jet-powered bomber. For seven years Boeing's designers and engineers laboured to create a bomber like no other. They were also keen to maintain their reputation as the preferred aircraft manufacturer for SAC, especially as the massive fifteen-man Convair B-36 Peacemaker, while impressive in some respects, fell short in others. It was too large to operate from most USAF airfields, limiting its operational flexibility, especially after the Soviets revealed their nuclear capabilities on 29 August 1949. SAC was immediately drawn into what would become a decades-long arms race between conventional and missile-powered deterrence, and the B-36 was too slow and too large to be an effective and easily deployable asset.

In the immediate post-war years, any development programme was hindered by the US Army Air Force (USAAF) and its successor, the USAF, being unable to determine how they envisioned air power being used in the nuclear age. This, in turn, hampered developments by aeronautical companies such as Boeing, who almost had to second-guess any USAAF doctrine. The result was frequent changes to both briefs and designs. Initial post-war ideas, made in November 1945, underwent numerous changes, so that by the end of 1948, specifications called for a 280,000-lbs (127,006kg) aircraft capable of carrying a 10,000-lbs (4,535kg) load, flying 6,909

miles (11,119km) at an altitude of 35,000ft (10.7km) and at a speed of 513mph (825km/h).

Boeing was partially ahead of the curve, having initiated the design process of what would become the B-52 on 13 February 1946 in response to a formal request for designs made in November 1945. The critical criteria of the request pointed to a next-generation intercontinental bomber to replace the Convair B-36, which had yet to enter service, let alone make its first flight. In response, Boeing, the Glenn L. Martin Company, and Consolidated-Vultee Aircraft Corporation submitted initial designs and cost estimates. Despite not meeting the desired combat radius, Boeing's Model 462 was selected as the winning bid on 5 June 1946 and was subsequently designated the XB-52, with the official contract awarded on 28 June.

With post-war austerity now affecting military aircraft development, like the situation during the development of the XB-15 over a decade earlier, Boeing found itself financially constrained by a budget of $1.7 million to cover the development of engines, weapons systems, structural testing, and a full-scale mock-up. The initial design resembled an XB-15 but was almost sixty per cent larger, at around 161ft (forty-nine metres) in length with a wingspan of 221ft (sixty-seven metres). It was to be powered by six Wright XT35 Typhoon turboprop engines, with the inner fairing housing the undercarriage. Despite its impressive appearance, the USAAF was concerned about the Model 462's size. Major General Earle Partridge, an experienced bomber commander and the Assistant Chief of Air Staff for Operations, pointed out that Boeing's efforts failed to meet the design brief.

Ever resilient, Boeing returned to the drawing board and created the Model 464, which would serve as the foundation for the B-52. The first iteration of the design, the Model 464, featured four Wright T35 engines and was lighter than the Model 462. At this point, General Curtis Le May, a B-29 veteran and Deputy Chief of the Air Staff for Research and Development, entered the picture at the end of 1946. Le May, known for his straightforward manner, argued that the B-52 would need to travel farther and faster. The USAAF requested a study focusing on a four-engine general-purpose bomber capable of carrying a special weapon 12,000 miles (19,312km) at a cruise speed of 400mph (644km/h).

Boeing responded with two separate models that they believed could meet the requirements: the 464-16, designed for the carriage of 10,000lbs (4,535kg) of special weapons, and the 464-17, designed for the carriage of 90,000lbs (40,823kg) of conventional weapons. The 464-17 was considered best suited to meet the USAAF's needs, despite its reduced range, which in-flight refuelling developments could

The Operation Crossroads ABLE test which took place on 1 July 1946 at Bikini Atoll, gives an impression of how powerful early special weapons were. (Library of Congress)

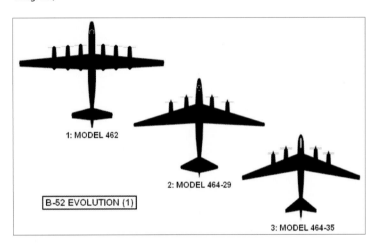

Evolution of the Boeing B-52 Stratofortress from Model 462 to Model 464-35. (Greg V. Goebel)

Major General Earle Partridge would become the Commanding General of the Special Weapons Command, directing SAC's nuclear options, of which the B-52 was to become a key vehicle for delivery. (Federal Civil Defense Administration)

overcome. Despite a positive result, Le May remained unsatisfied with the 464-17's size and cost. His concerns were echoed by Major General Laurence Craigie from the

LeMay (centre), with Brigadier General Lauris Norstad, on the left, and Brigadier General Thomas Power in March 1945, understood that good design, combined with great crews, made excellent bombers; an approach he would adopt in the B-52's use. (US Government (National Archives)

Boeing had learned a great deal from the Second World War, including the design, development, and building of cutting-edge aircraft; the B-52 would be as innovative as its predecessors. (Andreas Feininger)

USAAF Engineering Division, who felt that the 464-17 was too like the B-36, making it susceptible to obsolescence before entering service. At this point, the entire project teetered on the edge of cancellation, but Le May pushed for an extension of the project. Boeing was granted six months to explore their options and investigate a design that would meet Air Force expectations.

Instead of starting from scratch, Boeing further developed their original design, and soon a succession of variations began to emerge from the design team in the early months of 1947. At this point, the design Boeing settled on was the 464-29. The 464-29 featured a host of refinements, including a wing with a twenty-degree sweepback and an extended tail. Boeing also adopted four fuselage-mounted twin-wheel landing gears, supplemented by outriggers housed in the outer engine fairings. However, the design had its drawbacks, as the new version weighed 400,000lbs (181,436kg) and had an operational radius of 5,000 miles (8,047km). During this redesign phase, the Air Materiel Command of the newly established USAF was tasked with exploring ways of carrying out a nuclear strike, a process that had the potential to derail Boeing's work.

The newly formed USAF was also keen to make its mark as an independent air force and established the Heavy Bombardment Committee (HBC). The HBC had been created to evaluate the long-range bomber programme to which the XB-15 belonged, and how best to ensure aircraft flying from the United States were adequately defended against ground-based air defence. It was a straightforward enough task, given that the primary weapons of anti-aircraft defences remained artillery and larger calibre machine guns and cannon. The HBC also refined the design brief further, focusing on delivering special weapons over 8,000 miles (12,875km) with aircraft maintaining a cruise speed of 550mph (885km/h). Once again, Boeing's offering was frustratingly obsolete, leaving it under threat of cancellation, which occurred on 11 December 1947. The reaction from Boeing was, unsurprisingly, disbelief mixed with anger. Boeing Chairman William Allen made representations to the Secretary of the Air Force, Stuart Symington, that bought Boeing and the Model 464 an eleventh-hour reprieve the following January. This was followed by further government wrangling while they considered the viability of Northrop's B-49 'Flying Wing,' which was over rather

rapidly, leaving Boeing with a revised contract that March. The new contract allowed Boeing to tailor their design to the revised military characteristics that came into effect the previous December. From that they unveiled the Model 464-35.

Although the USAF was aware of the Model 464-35 in early 1948, it wasn't formally submitted until April as part of Boeing's bid for inclusion in Phase II selections. Phase II would see the Model 464-35's design, development, manufacture, and flight characteristics thoroughly tested through two XB-52s. The Model 464-35 featured a further sweep back of the wings, now with a span of 185ft (56m). The four Wright T35 engines were now fitted with contra-rotating propellers, giving the XB-52 a maximum speed of approximately 500mph (805km/h). The overall airframe was smaller, measuring 131ft (40m) in length, and the weight was reduced to 280,000lbs (127,006kg). It was clear Boeing was now making headway and getting closer to the original 1947 brief.

On 24 June 1948 the Soviets closed all land routes into Berlin, forcing the West to establish an air bridge. The subsequent airlift showed that the Soviets had underestimated the power of air resupply and the West's determination not to be cowed into submission. The political fallout of what was to be the first significant event of the Cold War soon filtered into military planning. By the time the blockade was lifted on 12 May 1949, the West had formed a new intergovernmental military alliance known as the North Atlantic Treaty Organization (NATO). SAC, whose position had been cemented as the vanguard of any US response in 1948, was now developing into a critical element of a broader NATO defence umbrella. Planners' minds,

Too advanced for its own good; the Northrop B-49 'Flying Wing' concept would have to undergo fifty years of development before being accepted into USAF service as the B-2. (American Aviation Historical Society)

Students from Humboldt University hold a demonstration on Dorotheenstrasse in partitioned Berlin, where the political atmosphere was becoming increasingly charged. (Bundesarchiv)

USAF C-47s parked in front of the terminal at Tempelhof Central Airport during the Berlin Airlift. (US Federal Government)

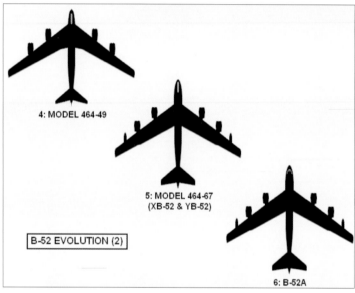

4: MODEL 464-49

5: MODEL 464-67 (XB-52 & YB-52)

B-52 EVOLUTION (2)

6: B-52A

The final evolution of the B-52. (Greg V. Goebel)

wandering for the previous three years, were now focused on the task at hand.

Meanwhile, Boeing had been lobbied by the USAF in May to transition to turbojets rather than turboprops. Aided by continuous technological developments leading to more powerful and economical engine designs, Boeing released the Model 464-40 in July. Influenced by the XB-47 that had made its maiden flight the previous December, Boeing unveiled an eight-engine airplane. The eight Westinghouse XJ40-WE-12 engines were paired in four underwing pods, which, on paper, gave the Model 464-40 superior performance, in terms of speed and altitude, than requested. Regardless of Boeing's considerable efforts, including putting their faith in new technology, the Deputy Chief of Staff for Materiel, Lieutenant General Howard Craig, remained unconvinced. Craig, who had previously directed the Air Materiel Command (AMC) to cancel the XB-52 programme, felt the turbojet was still developing and considered it a power source for future bombers. The turboprop

was better suited to contemporary designs. Despite Craig's misgivings, Boeing was contacted by Colonel Henry Warden of AMC Wright Air Development Centre. Warden had been a critical point of contact between Boeing and the USAF during the XB-52 programme. Warden convened a meeting at Wright-Patterson AFB, Ohio, between Boeing's engineering team and himself on 21 October 1948. The aim was to discuss the accepted Model 464-35 design rather than a Turbojet design. The Boeing team must have been dismayed, as the toing-and-froing from the USAF must now have been beyond frustrating. The Boeing team, consisting of Edward Wells, George Schairer, Vaughn Blumenthal, Harold Withington, Art Carlsen, and Maynard Pennell, maintained their dignity and considered Warden's suggestions despite them flying in the face of Craig's recent comments as the team retreated to the Van Cleve Hotel in Dayton, Ohio, for the weekend of 23–24 October to reconsider their designs and factor in turbojets once more, doing so in ignorant bliss of what Warden had been doing in the background.

At this stage, and unbeknown to Boeing or the AMC, Warden effectively acted on his own authority when he sent the Boeing team away to redesign the XB-52. Warden was also aware that Pratt and Whitney, at his request, had been pushing ahead with the development of their JT3 Turbojet. Over the following weekend, the team, who had informed Warden they would have a fresh proposal ready the following Monday, drew up the plans for the basic design of what we would recognize today as the B-52. The new design would include turbojets rather than turboprops.

Drawing on their work from the XB-47 project and an in-house medium bomber exercise, the team created a new airplane, which was to be the Model 464-49. The team had worked hard, taking the best attributes of the XB-47 and the

A USAF inspector observes NBC-clad members of a combat logistics support squadron replacing a damaged Pratt & Whitney J57 engine of a B-52D during exercise Night Train/Global Shield 1984 at Davis-Monthan AFB, Arizona. (Technical Sergeant Rob Marshall. USAF)

medium bomber exercise, doubling them, refining the figures, working the data, and delivering a feasible model. Like the Model 464-40, the Model 464-49 featured eight engines paired together in four underwing pods, this time using Pratt and Whitney J57s, the military equivalent of the J3. The new design would weigh approximately 330,000lbs (149,685kg), have a radius of 3,061 miles (4,926km) at speeds of 564mph (908km/h), and carry a 10,000-lbs (4,535kg) payload. Another noticeable difference was the redesigned wing with an increased chord and a sweep of thirty-five degrees, which gave the Model 464-49 an impressive wing area of 4,000 square feet (1,219 square metres). While one team worked hard to produce a thirty-three-page study, another created a scale model of the proposal from supplies bought at a local hobby store.

The Boeing team's subsequent presentation convinced Warden, and the Model 464-49 showed what was possible. While Warden remained confident that the turbojet was the way ahead, the USAF remained unsure until January 1949 when the USAF Board of Senior Officers formally released a study fully endorsing jet propulsion for bombers. This was confirmed on 26 January when Boeing was given an amendment to their existing contract to develop the Model 464-49. Boeing was now free to let loose on their new design, and on 26 April, an inspection of their mock-up at Seattle by USAF personnel finally took place. It was the first mock-up of the process thus far to be inspected by the USAF. It represented a milestone in the development of the XB-52. While the USAF was now formally pushing Pratt and Whitney to refine their engines Boeing sought more technical means to increase the XB-52's range, delivering a

further refinement with the Model 464-67 in November 1949. Although 60,000lbs (27,216kg) heavier, the new combat radius was calculated to be 4,356mi (6,978km) on serial production XB-52s.

The inspection went well, and Boeing's work was well received. Still, they were left with range and engine development issues. In October, Major General Orville Cook of the AMC pushed for another revision of the military characteristics. At this point, LeMay, who had taken command of SAC from General George Kenney in

The XB-52 on the ground clearly showing her tandem cockpit inherited from the B-47 and soon changed to a more conventional arrangement after pressure from LeMay, among others. (American Aviation Historical Society)

The YB-52 takes off from Boeing Field. The B-52 is starting to take shape. (American Aviation Historical Society)

The YB-52 in flight. By now, all the key components were in place for serial production. (American Aviation Historical Society)

October 1948, pushed for further engine development, keenly aware that additional engineering and technical development would improve the range. He also convened a conference of all the key agencies and personalities involved in developing the XB-52 to study the programme's progress.

LeMay's conference took place in late January 1950, where the agenda now looked at alternatives alongside the overall progress of the XB-52. Convair proposed a swept-wing, turbojet-powered B-36G, later becoming the YB-60. In contrast, others, including Douglas and Fairchild, presented their ideas, echoing the B-47's appearance. LeMay was far from impressed, and the

XB-52 continued its development as a strategic bomber unhindered. A month after the meeting, LeMay pushed Model 464-67 to replace Model 464-49, which remained the officially endorsed design. LeMay's lobbying was successful, and on 24 March 1950, the Model 464-67 replaced the Model 464-49 as the officially endorsed bomber design. Despite this seemingly momentous moment, Boeing's work was yet to be ordered into serial production. For almost a year, nothing appeared to be happening. In some quarters of the USAF the discussion remained how the B-52 would be used more effectively as a bomber or reconnaissance asset, thus meeting SAC's desire to have a dual-use aircraft. This conversation would continue into 1951, when, in October, a directive was issued that would, in effect, turn all B-52s into RB-52s. The B-52, as the bomber, was suddenly redundant. Ultimately, the dual-use arrangement won the day, and the B-52 would see the use of reconnaissance pods in the RB-52B and C models.

For almost 12 months, the sideline lobbying continued by Convair for their YB-60. Still, SAC's belief that the B-52 was by far the most adaptable design ensured the programme remained alive. However, events in Southeast Asia and declining East-West relations gave LeMay a veritable ace card. With the advent of the Korean War, he argued for SAC fleet modernization, amply supported by Second World War-vintage B-29s being used to support operations. LeMay knew that the B-52 would be the vanguard of this modernization. On 9 January 1951, General Hoyt Vandenberg, USAF Chief of Staff, approved the B-52 as the replacement for the B-36 for SAC. This was followed by an endorsement on 24 January from Thomas Finletter, Secretary of the Air Force, that led to a contract confirming the move to serial production. On 14 February, representatives from Boeing and the USAF signed the contract,

Above: The Convair YB-60, a swept-wing jet-powered derivative of the B-36 at Edwards AFB with a B-36F in the background. (National Museum of the US Air Force)

Left: The RB-52B 52-0008 in flight, showing its rear fuselage design and lack of defensive armament. (USAF)

and production began for the first thirteen B-52As, scheduled for delivery in April 1953.

Boeing's Plant 2 in Seattle, Washington, commenced with two pre-production models, the XB-52 and the YB-52. These were exclusively Boeing-built, making them the only two B-52s of their kind. They featured several variations compared to the final series production models, most notably the B-47-styled tandem cockpit for the pilots. This arrangement, however, would be short-lived, as Boeing reverted to the more conventional side-by-side seating arrangement for the pilots from the A model onwards.

Planning to produce the B-52 presented Boeing with a massive manufacturing challenge, akin to the construction of the B-29 during the Second World War and the B-47, Boeing's first-generation turbojet bomber. The experiences gained from building these two aeroplanes would assist Boeing immensely, but challenges persisted, including the need to introduce the B-52 into squadron service. Nearly 5,000 sub-contractors were assigned, and by the advent of the D model, they were supplying approximately one-third of an individual B-52's mass through the assembly of sub-assemblies and the supply of critical components. Sub-contractors such as Goodyear provided fuselage fuel cells, and Fairchild supplied the tail fin and outer wing sections, while Boeing retained responsibility for manufacturing the front fuselage, inner wing, and inner leading-edge structures. Despite this approach,

Below: The new kid on the block. The XB-52 faces off against the old guard in 1955. (US Government)

Bottom: B-36s pictured at Carswell AFB, Texas, 24 April 1949. Even at this point the B-36 was nearing obsolescence, highlighting the urgency for SAC to develop its next-generation heavy bomber. (E. W. Weinberger/ USAF)

Boeing required additional manufacturing space and later established the Wichita production line in Kansas to help share the load. The Wichita production line did not produce its first B-52 until June 1956.

On 29 November 1951, the XB-52 rolled off the production lines. Due to security concerns there was no fanfare as the new bomber first saw the light of day in the dead of night, concealed by a vast shroud of fabric. However, due to an almost catastrophic pneumatic-system testing failure and subsequent rebuild during the ground testing phase, one of the eight phases that the XB-52 and YB-52 would face, the maiden flight of the XB-52 did not occur until 2 October 1952. The YB-52 fared better and was rolled out of the assembly halls on 15 March 1952, making her maiden flight on 15 April. It was piloted by Boeing's test pilot, Alvin 'Tex' Johnson, who later gained fame for barrel-rolling the

367-80 jet airliner prototype, and Lieutenant Colonel Guy Townsend from the USAF's Air Research and Development Command. The new aeroplane received very few negative remarks, despite one of the landing gear units failing to retract correctly, defects with the liquid oxygen supply, and stiff controls that were later adjusted to minimize pilot fatigue. Subsequent tests showed that the Boeing design team had created a winning aeroplane. The YB-52, tested at Moses Lake AFB, Washington, returned to Boeing Field after just a week of flight testing. By October 1952, the team had logged fifty hours of flight time, and despite pushing hard, the testing schedule was beginning to slip. On the plus side, the YB-52 was joined by the XB-52 on 2 October, which expedited the Phase I testing cycle. By November, the two aeroplanes had commenced Phase II testing. Between 3 November and 15 March 1953, Boeing worked tirelessly to complete the tests and attempt to regain lost ground in the testing schedule.

Interestingly, Boeing persuaded the USAF that testing in Washington would be more advantageous than relocating to the Air Force Flight Test Centre (AFFTC) at Edwards AFB, California. Boeing argued that if any remedial work was required, then Seattle would be the best place to do it, where all the equipment and expertise were available. It also allowed around 600 Boeing staff to evaluate the millions of pieces of data from each flight in familiar territory. The AFFTC was supported by the Air Research and Development Command (ARDC), which possessed premier testing facilities. Surprisingly, the AMC initially supported Boeing, if only to keep the testing costs low. However, it was Seattle's changeable weather that led to delays in 1953, prompting the USAF to change its stance. The testing programme was moved

to Moses Lake AFB, among other USAF sites on the continental United States, including the AFFTC. Other USAF sites used in the testing phase included the all-important Air Proving Ground Command, Eglin AFB, Florida, and the Air Development Centre at Wright-Patterson AFB, Ohio.

While most of Phase II, primarily conducted by the YB-52, proceeded without significant issues, the J37 engines, essentially prototypes, raised considerable concerns. They experienced high-altitude surges during normal throttle-control exercises, raising fears of potential flameouts. Other areas of concern included an inadequate braking system and a starboard pitch-up and roll when approaching the stall. Phase III, which was used for contractor development testing, began in late March 1953. The XB-52, which had recently returned to service, took the lead, but was soon grounded and remained so for over a year.

Phase IV focused on performance and stability, with over 200 flight hours flown to generate a comprehensive evaluation.

Phase V examined the B-52's all-weather capabilities and involved visits to the famed McKinley Laboratory at Eglin AFB, where airframes were subjected to extremes of heat and cold. The latter tests proved invaluable in the early stages of the B-52's operational career when sorties were frequently flown out of Alaska and around the Arctic Circle. As Phase V testing continued, the B-52A finally made its maiden flight on 5 August 1954, followed by the unveiling of the first production RB-52Bs in December of the same year.

The new A models took part in Phase VI testing, which evaluated the weapons systems, including the all-important Fire Control Systems, defence systems, and reconnaissance pods. In addition to the forward crew area, there was a galley for preparing hot meals, a rest bunk, and a toilet. Tests were carried out in the final production configuration and flown by experienced SAC aircrew from the 90rd Bomb Wing based at Castle AFB, California. One aircraft was detailed to operate out of the USAF Special Weapons

Top: Personnel gather in front of a B-52H. The dip of the wings is noticeable, with the tips able to flex 6ft (180cm), up or down, from the horizontal aspect. Note the supporting wing wheels. (Mizzoujp)

Above: On 5 August 1954, the hitherto hidden B-52A with a reworked cockpit arrangement made its first flight. Note the absence of wing-mounted fuel tanks. (American Aviation Historical Society)

Above: A wonderful profile study of the B-52A at Pima Air & Space Museum, Arizona. (Aeroprints)

Right: The cockpit of the B-52D showing the dials for the eight J37 engines in the upper centre of the console and corresponding throttles below. Note the stowed anti-flash blinds. (National Museum of the US Air Force)

Centre at Kirtland AFB, New Mexico. It tested inert special-weapon-delivery system designs to collect ballistic and simulated operational data. In May 1956, the same B-52 (52-0013) would drop the first US thermonuclear special weapon, albeit twenty-one seconds early, near Namu Island at the Bikini Atoll as part of the Redwing Cherokee test, which was part of the wider Operation Cherokee series of tests. The same B-52 (52-0013) would later participate in the Pacific-based Operation Dominic tests designed to respond to the Soviet resumption of their nuclear testing programme.

This was followed, understandably, by Phase VII Operational Suitability testing and finally Phase VIII Unit Operational Employments tests, both conducted by SAC aircrew. Given the urgent requirement to make the B-52 operational, some phases overlapped. Testing was by no means over,

and numerous tests would be performed over the coming years as the role of the B-52 developed and technologies changed. In March 1954, the first of the A models were rolled out and accepted into service by SAC in June before being returned to Boeing for further testing. Overall, Boeing's testing process went exceptionally well, demonstrating that it had designed and constructed an outstanding aeroplane. There were still issues, particularly with fuelling, that would be addressed through the Blue Band, Hard Shell, and Quickclip projects. Snags with the Pratt and Whitney J57 turbojets and the bicycle undercarriage would also be ironed out over time.

In the summer of 1955, over two years behind schedule, the first squadron-ready B-52s rolled off the production lines and into the hands of a very grateful Strategic Air Command.

On 17 January 1966, a B-52G collided with a KC-135 during refuelling. The B-52 was carrying four B28FI Mod 2 Y1 thermonuclear (hydrogen) special weapons. All four were recovered, and two are on display at the National Museum of Nuclear Science & History, Albuquerque, New Mexico. (Marshall Astor)

As shown in this photograph, the B-52's bicycle landing gear is a marvel of engineering. (Carlos Menendez)

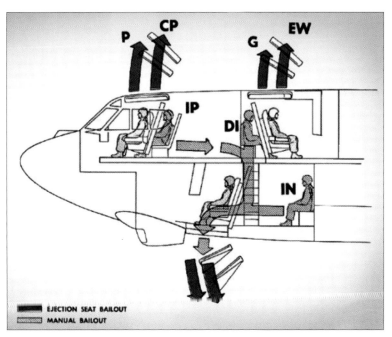

The revised cockpit design also necessitated the redesign of the crew escape routes via hatches and ejection seats, including temporary positions for the Instructor Pilot (IP), Defence Instructor (DI), and Instructor Navigator (IN). (Unknown)

B-52 Production Models

Colonel Paul Tibbets IV (left) takes a closer look at the nose art on a 93rd Bomb Squadron B-52H, at Barksdale AFB, Louisiana, which resembles the nose art on the side of a B-17 his grandfather flew in the Second World War.

Boeing would produce eight key models of the B-52, from unveiling the first B-52A on 18 March 1954 to the roll-out of the final B-52H on 26 October 1962. The production of the 744 B-52 airframes would be split between Boeing's base in Seattle and, later, its Wichita facility in Kansas. Only the A, B and C models were produced in Seattle. Wichita joined production for the D, E and F models in October 1955 before Seattle closed its production line. This left Wichita as the sole Boeing facility producing B-52s from late 1958, running serial production of the G and H models until 1962. In total, 467 B-52s would be built at Boeing's Wichita facility.

B-52A

Like its stablemate almost twenty years before, Boeing rolled out its first serial production B-52 with great aplomb despite producing only three airframes. The A model, of which only three airframes would be made in the summer of 1954, was initially delivered to the USAF before being returned to Boeing for flight testing. Despite lacking specific systems that in-service airframes would require for Strategic Air Command

Service (SAC), they served to help SAC pilots familiarize themselves with the type and serve as evaluation aeroplanes.

Compared to the YB-52 and XB-52, the B-52's primary physical change was the forward fuselage. Gone was the B-47-style tandem cockpit, replaced by the more familiar side-by-side cockpit that the previous Fortresses had enjoyed. This change was mainly driven by LeMay, who, as the head of SAC, was perhaps the most influential voice at the B-52's development table and preferred the more traditional side-by-side arrangement. The new cockpit arrangement was added to an already lengthened forward fuselage section, with the additional 21in (533mm) accommodating additional avionics and an extra crew member, bringing the crew to six.

The crew now consisted of a pilot, co-pilot, navigator, radar navigator, electronic warfare officer, and gunner. Like the B-29 and B-50, the gunner was separated from the rest of the crew during a pressurized flight. Overall, the gunner on the A to F models was restricted from moving between his station at the rear fuselage and the rest

Wichita was no stranger to building larger aircraft, as demonstrated in this wartime photograph of its B-29 production line, and it would soon get to grips with the B-52. (United States Army Air Forces)

Below: The crew of a B-52F returning from Operation Arc Light, note the bombs painted on the fuselage signifying the number of missions flown. (USAF)

of the crew at the front fuselage, mainly because the airframe was pressurized. He could move between his post and the front fuselage if the aircraft were depressurized or flying below 10,000ft (3,045.8m). To do so, however, he would have had to crawl along the right longeron and through several small bulkhead doors. This manoeuvre was hard enough on the ground, so at altitude, with an air bottle and in full flight gear, it would have been nearly impossible.

The A model was the first to be armed with a defensive armament, having four M-3 .50-cal guns mounted in the tail barbette, with each weapon fed with 600 rounds. The gunner was given the Bosch Arma A-3A Fire Control System (FSC); the B-52 was the first to be equipped with this particular system. The A-3A featured a tracking radar array capable of automatically laying and firing the gun battery. Using a periscope, the gunner could also manually lay the guns and fire them on target. Interestingly, as a flying test bed, the A model lacked any bombing navigational systems, and mission-specific avionics.

The A model was fitted with the more powerful Pratt & Whitney J57-P-1W engines, which allowed for water injection, increasing thrust levels from 10,000lbs 'dry' to 11,000lbs 'wet'. While the period for water injection was strictly limited to prevent engine damage, it significantly boosted the heavily laden B-52 operating in hot environments. With the water injection system, the B-52A, in particular, lost some of the fuel capacity the prototypes enjoyed. The wing recovered some of this loss of capacity by mounting 1,000-gallon (4,546-litre) fuel tanks, which appear to be seldom

A close-up of the four M3 .50-cal guns of the tail turret, seen here on a B-52D at USAF Academy, Colorado. (Greg Goebel)

fitted, leaving the aeroplane to rely on air-to-air refuelling.

The B-52A flew between 18 March 1954 and 1960. Two aircraft were assigned to other tasks, one becoming the NB-52 captive-carry and launch mothership, the other moving to the Technical Training Centre at Chanute Air Force Base, Illinois,

as a grounded teaching aid. The remaining A model was scrapped at Tinker in 1961.

B-52B

The B model was to become the first serial production B-52, with the delivery of the first airframe, an RB-52B (*see* Variants), to the 93rd Bomb Wing at Castle Air Force

A B-52H deploying its braking parachute at Barksdale AFB, Louisiana. (Kevin Jackson)

A close-up of the main landing gear of the Duxford Air Museum's B-52D in England. (Chad Kainz)

A wonderfully marked-up early B-52B from Castle AFB, California; note the white belly and rear fuselage SAC stripe. (American Aviation Historical Society)

A crew scrambles to their RB-52B at March AFB, California, 1965. This aircraft was assigned to the 22nd Bombardment Wing. (USAF)

Six AGM-86Bs ALCMs are raised into position ready for fitting to the wing of this B-52G at Fairchild AFB, Washington. (Staff Sergeant Bob Simons)

Base (AFB), taking place in late June 1955. The key driver for how the new aeroplane would operate could be found in an Air Staff directive released in October four years earlier. The message was clear: the new aeroplane would be a reconnaissance type first, and a bomber second. This decision led to two distinct production types: the B and the RB-52B, which would carry a particular reconnaissance pod. This would shape the future use as a platform throughout the early phases of development, with the Air Staff suddenly about-facing a mere two weeks before the maiden flight of the first B model. This sudden change of heart must have been seen as chaotic, especially given the fact that over half of the B model production run was to be the reconnaissance type.

That aside, the A model test phase had helped, as both B models were identical in most respects. The initial production models featured Pratt & Whitney J57-P-1W engines with improvements to water injection. Later engines would include J57-P-29W and J57-P-29WA, which were fitted while Pratt & Whitney struggled to overcome difficulties working with titanium. These were overcome with titanium compressor blades fitted to the J57-P-19W, a development of the J57-P-1W fitted to the final five production B models. Remarkably, the thrust rating for 19W, 29W, and 29WA engines was precisely the same, with a dry thrust of 10,500lbs (4762,72kg) and a wet thrust of 12,100lbs (5488,47kg).

Other challenges included avionics, with the bombing, navigation, and fire

Top: Watched by ground crew, this early B-52 arrives at Edwards AFB, California. (American Aviation Historical Society)

Above: A B-52 in Climate Laboratory Hangar Cold Weather Testing at Eglin AFB, Florida. (USAF)

An interesting close-up of the engine inlets on the Duxford Air Museum B-52D. (Chad Kainz)

control systems all remaining problematic, especially the unpredictable IBM MA-2 BRANE (Bombing Radar Navigation Equipment) bombing-navigation system (BNS). Such were the concerns of SAC that it was decided to use the Sperry-Rand K-3A bombing and navigation system, as fitted in the Convair B-36. This system allowed a single crew member to act as radar operator and bombardier. While a reliable system, the K-3A could not operate efficiently above 35,000ft (10,668m), and given the B-52 was expected to perform above 45,000ft (13,716m), the fix needed to be more suitable. The key issues with the K-3A were its poor resolution and definition qualities. Philco, then the leading specialists in high-frequency transistor development, provided a temporary fix to increase output until the arrival of the Sperry-Rand MA-6A, essentially an upgraded K-3A.

During the testing of the A model, issues were found with the tail FCS; to that end, Boeing fitted differing systems. The original Bosch Arma A-3A was fitted to the first nine RB-52Bs with a Bosch Arma MD-5 FCS, which used a pair of M24A-1 20mm cannon, fitted to the following thirty-four B models. This system proved equally unreliable, so Boeing fitted the remaining seven B models with an improved A-3A FCS, which saw the reintroduction of the four M-3 .50-cal guns.

All B models would be delivered to the 93rd Bomb Wing at Castle AFB, with some airframes seeing service well into the 1960s, with final retirement between 1955 and 1966. With the implementation of the dispersal policy, to counter mass force loss from a nuclear attack, the B models would be sent to the 95th Bomb Wing at Biggs AFB, Texas, and the 22nd Bomb Wing at March AFB, California.

The B model was a limited production run with fifty airframes made, with the dual-purpose RB-52B bomber/reconn-aissance

A dramatic shot showing a lightning strike behind a B-52H at Minot AFB, North Dakota. (Senior Airman Justin Armstrong)

A wonderful image of an B-52C assembly taking place at Seattle. (AF GlobalStrike).

planes comprising twenty-seven of the aircraft delivered. A single B model would be transferred to NASA as the NB-52B captive-carry and launch mothership 'Balls Eight', finally retiring in 2004. Project Sunflower would see seven B models converted to the B-52C standard.

B-52C

Only thirty-five C models were built at Seattle, which flew for the first time on 9 March 1956 and entered service with the 42nd Bomb Wing at Loring AFB, Maine, the following June. Like the B models, the C was a dual reconnaissance/bomber aeroplane, but the RB designation was eschewed for the C despite it being able to carry the two-man reconnaissance pod. The C model featured further refinements as aircrews and engineers perfected the aeroplane; the key noticeable difference, retro-applied to those B models still in service, was the white, anti-flash underside. The other was upgrading the wing-mounted 1,000-gallon (4,546-litre) fuel tanks to the massive 3,000-gallon (13,638-litre) types. Despite the apparent weight gain, the C model retained the Pratt & Whitney J57-P-19W and J57-P-29W.

In terms of systems management, very little changed, with the Bosch Arma A-3A FCS retained for all but one C model, which

Two former ground crew members walk towards the B52-A at The National Museum of Nuclear Science & History in Albuquerque, New Mexico, which dropped the first Mk-15 thermonuclear special weapon over the Bikini Atoll in May 1956. (MikeMcBey)

was the last production model and was fitted with an improved Bosch Arma MD-9 FCS. A new AN/ASQ-48 bombing and navigation system would later be retrofitted into the C model fleet as it was added to D models.

After squadron service with the 99th Bomb Wing at Westover AFB, Massachusetts, the C fleet would be redistributed among

Now carrying a complete fuselage, the construction of the B-52C is moved outside, note the folded tail. (AF GlobalStrike).

The B-25D was the first of the B-52s to enter volume serial production. (US Government)

D model units, remaining in service until 1971 when they were consigned to storage.

B-52D

The D series of B-52s were the first to be jointly constructed between Boeing's plants at Seattle and Wichita in Kansas. The first D model to fly was a Wichita aeroplane, taking to the skies on 14 May 1956. A little over four months later, Seattle's first D would leave the plant on 28 September. The D was similar to the C model, but what made it different was its distinct role as a bomber; SAC were no longer sitting on the fence regarding this matter. The world was changing; thus, the B-52's role and future missions were clearly defined.

The production of the D model was further helped by the fact that two plants were manufacturing it, with aeroplanes reaching flight lines by the autumn of 1956. The D was a successful model and subjected to modifications during its service life, including upgrades to its bombing capacity. The D models continued providing conventional and nuclear strike capacities into the 1980s, with examples serving alongside, and outliving, the E and F models.

Of the 170 D models built, Seattle produced 101 airframes, with Wichita producing sixty-nine.

B-52E

The production of the E model saw the main effort of B-52 production shift from Seattle to Wichita, which would produce fifty-eight of the 100 airframes ordered. Seattle delivered the first E to SAC on 3 October 1957, with Wichita following two weeks later, on 14 October. Serial production airframes were handed over to SAC throughout the following December. Externally, the E closely resembled the D, but its avionics had changed due to SAC's continual modification of its bomber doctrine, heavily influenced by the Soviet Union. The Soviets were catching up with NATO, particularly the United States, regarding nuclear weapon capacity and delivery. Another critical development was the Soviet air defence system, initially

B-52Ds sit on Seattle's flightline undergoing work on their J57s. Of note is the early anti-flash white belly, that would eventually be painted black. (AF GlobalStrike).

Little and large; a Wichita B-52D stands behind a Model 75 Kaydet trainer. (AF GlobalStrike).

An intriguing view of Lieutenant Reed Elsbernd, 20th Bomb Squadron, flying a B-52H during a Green Flag-East training mission on 21 August 2013, Fort Polk, Louisiana. (Staff Sergeant Jonathan Snyder)

A B-52E on a low-level test flight in less-than-ideal flying conditions, testing the new SAC doctrine. (USAF)

Looking towards the nose from the bomb bay of a B-52H of the 96th Bomb Squadron, 2nd Bomb Wing, Barksdale AFB, Louisiana. (Robert Frola)

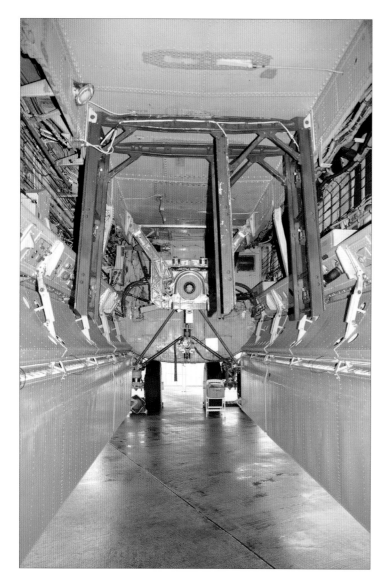

considered foolproof due to its high level of interoperability between all elements, although this was later disproved.

The SAC firmly believed that the high altitudes at which the B-52 was intended to operate were now compromised. After evaluation, the decision was made to start operating at a lower level. With the gift of altitude and its relatively safe environment gone, crews now had to learn how to deal with the hazards of low-altitude flying. Such tactics also required new avionics, and the E model was the first B-52 to be equipped with IBM's AN/ASQ-38 Computer, Altitude Vertical Velocity. The AN/ASQ-38 was designed to be an accurate and reliable weapons system for the new working method. As with all new systems, there were plenty of initial issues, primarily related to performance and maintenance.

These early issues were eventually rectified, but the urgency of the fix became the subject of the Jolly Well programme, which was finally completed in 1964. The fixes would be expensive, as they affected the E model fleet and the following models up to and including the H model, with 480 B-52s affected overall.

The E model had a relatively short service life, with the first examples retiring in 1967, and most being placed into storage between 1969 and 1970.

B-52F

The F model, the last of the 'Tall Tail' models, was also the final B-52 model to be produced in Seattle, with the first example leaving the plant on 6 May 1958. It was followed by the Wichita plant's first F model on 14 May, with serial deliveries taking place between June 1958 and February 1959. The critical difference between the F model and its predecessor was the installation of Pratt & Whitney's new 'dash 43' engines, known as the J57-P-43-W, J57-P-43-WA, and J57-P-43-WB. These engines produced 11,200lbs of dry thrust and 13,750lbs of wet thrust.

In addition to increased power, the new engines supplied the aircraft with all of its electrical power by incorporating alternators. Fitted to the port-side pod of each engine pair, the new alternators did away with the problematic fuselage-mounted air-driven turbines and alternators fitted to previous models. With this change, there was a noticeable redesign of the engine cowling covers, which gave the port engines a noticeable bulge on the

A B-52F carrying a pair of the North American Aviation AGM-28 Hound Dog on its underwing pylons. (US Government)

lower port side of the nacelle. Small ram air intakes were also added to the lower lip of the air intakes to provide cooling for the engine oil and constant-speed drives.

The F model also benefited from an increase in its conventional load capacity. This was tested by F models of the 7th and 320th Bomb Wings, which became the first B-52s to bomb targets in South Vietnam in June 1965. The F began its withdrawal from service in 1967, with more following between 1969 and 1973, and the final lot retired in 1978. Seattle completed forty-four of the eighty-nine F models finally produced, while Wichita built forty-five.

B-52G

The G model saw the B-52 make another leap forward. Not only would it be produced solely by the Wichita plant, but it would also feature a range of design changes. The G became the most numerous of the 744 B-52s, with 193 examples built between 1958 and 1961. The first G flew on 31 August 1958, with the first production aircraft entering service with the 5th Bomb Wing at Travis AFB, California, in February 1959, and the final aircraft delivered almost two years later.

The G was almost an entirely new aircraft. Boeing and SAC were keen to reduce structural weight. The G had its take-off weight increased to a staggering 488,000lbs (221,353kg), with much of the increased weight coming from the G's ability to carry more fuel, 48,030 gallons compared to 41,563gal (157,333l) carried by its predecessor. Most of the additional fuel

The B-52F is rolled out and ready for delivery to SAC. Note the folded tail to allow the exit from the assembly hall. (US Government)

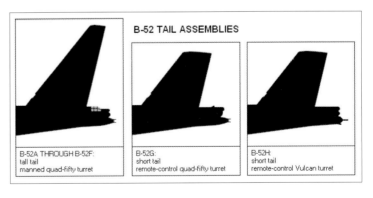

B-52 TAIL ASSEMBLIES

B-52A THROUGH B-52F:
tall tail
manned quad-fifty turret

B-52G:
short tail
remote-control quad-fifty turret

B-52H:
short tail
remote-control Vulcan turret

was held in a new 'wet wing', the design of which would later give Boeing and the USAF problems. Despite the weight gain, the new amounts of fuel carried increased range and combat radius and were welcomed with open arms. As a result of the increased internal fuel weight, the wing-mounted

The many tails of the B-52. These silhouettes show how much the final models of the B-52 changed. (Greg V. Goebel)

Right: The B-52G is rolled out featuring a new tail and a host of other innovations. (American Aviation Historical Society)

Below: A unique photograph of B-52Gs arranged and ready for quick response. Note the KC-135 tanker in the background. (AF Global Strike)

Bottom: An interesting photograph of an early B-52G taken in October 1958. Note the B-47 Chase Plane and the blister on the lower rear fuselage. (American Aviation Historical Society)

3,000-gal (11,356l) fuel tanks were changed to smaller 700-gal (2,650l) tanks.

The structural weight reduction was achieved by using new alloys during the construction phase, alongside the redesign of certain elements, the most obvious of which was the reduction in the size of the vertical fin. Further weight was saved by moving the gunner from the aft of the fuselage and seating him next to the Electronic Warfare Officer in the forward fuselage section. This new position also afforded the gunner an ejection seat.

A new Fire Control System (FCS) was fitted with an Avco-Crosley AN/ASG-15 Defensive Fire Control System, which utilized different radar dishes for search and track functions. Initially, the AN/ASG-15 was also fitted with a television camera, though the AN/ALQ-117 system later replaced this. The US Dynamics AN/ALQ-117 active countermeasures set was mounted in pairs on the rear of the aft fuselage, working as a noise/deception jamming system. This was later updated to the PAVE MINT configuration, alongside the H model, in a programme started in 1981. Despite the upgrade in FCS and the increase in space with the relocation of the gunner, the rear armament remained unchanged. However, it allowed Boeing to move the storage location for the 44ft (13m) braking parachute to the top of the aft fuselage section.

In terms of offensive capabilities, the G model was, once again, more powerful than its predecessors as it became the first B-52 to possess a standoff capacity. The first weapon carried this way was the North American GAM-77, later known as the AGM-28, Hound Dog. The GAM-77 was a supersonic, turbojet-propelled, nuclear-armed, air-launched nuclear-capable cruise missile capable of achieving Mach 2.1 (1,611mph/2,593km/h) in flight. The fit for the GAM-77 didn't start until the fifty-fifth airframe was built, with the previous fifty-four airframes being retrofitted to carry and launch the missile.

Additionally, the G model carried the McDonnell Aircraft Corporation GAM-72 Quail, a subsonic-cruise unarmed decoy (SCUD), later known as the ADM-20. The GAM-72 was a purpose-designed subsonic, jet-powered, air-launched decoy cruise missile for the B-52. Four GAM-72s were carried internally and contained suitable electronics and radar reflectors, making it indistinguishable from an approaching, low-altitude B-52. The intent was to force Soviet air defences to divide their assets

The first fully camouflaged B-52G sits on the flight line of the 92nd Bombardment Wing at Fairchild AFB, Washington. (Staff Sergeant Bob Simons)

between multiple targets, thus increasing the B-52's survivability while wasting the Soviet's defensive resources.

The G equipped eleven squadrons and began to be withdrawn from service starting in May 1989, with a gradual withdrawal from service completed in May 1994.

B-52H

The H model was the final, and many say the finest, expression of the B-52. Referred to as the Cadillac, a brand synonymous with luxury, the H, which flew for the first time on 6 March 1961, was fitted with Pratt & Whitney TF33-P-3 turbo-fan engines. The eight TF33-P-3s made an immediate difference in appearance to the H, with the turbo-fan cowlings standing proud at the front of the engine; they also made a big difference to the performance of the H. The new engine fit gave the H an increased power rating of 17,000lbs and an increase in combat radius to 4,806 miles (8,900km) with a 10,000lbs (4,536kg) ordnance load. The new engines were also cleaner, quieter, and more economical, improving crew comfort on flights and giving the H greater operational flexibility since distilled water was no longer required for the deployment of the type.

Another critical design change saw the defensive tail armament changed from the four .50-cal guns to a single General Electric M61A1 Vulcan multi-barrelled 20mm rotary cannon. This was fed by a 1,242-round magazine and used an Emerson AN/ASG-21 B-52H Defensive Fire Control System, which consisted of dual search and tracking radar to lay the guns on target. While impressive on paper, the AN/ASG-21 could only focus on one target at a time, and the gunner remained with the rest of the crew in the forward fuselage. The M61A1 stayed with the H model until its fleet-wide removal in 1991.

Like the G model, the H was also equipped to carry the AGM-28 and similar gravity weapon loads, both nuclear and conventional. It would be fitted to carry Boeing's AGM-69 SRAM (Short-Range Attack Missile) nuclear-armed

A heavily weathered Boeing B-52D that forms part of a small collection of aircraft commemorating the former K. I. Sawyer AFB near Gwinn, Michigan. (Steve Fine)

air-to-surface missile from 1972 and the subsonic AGM-86B ALCM (Air-Launched Cruise Missile) from 1982. The H was also equipped to carry four Douglas GAM-87 Skybolt (AGM-48) hypersonic ALBMs (Air-Launched Ballistic Missiles), which would have taken a W59 thermonuclear warhead. GAM-87 soon became a shared

A 456th Bombardment Wing, Boeing B-52G-85-BW Stratofortress (57-6491), Beale AFB, California. Note the GAM-77 Hound Dog under its wing. (US Government)

An early B-52G with a GAM-72 Quail in the foreground. (AF Global Strike)

This B-52H would have two names in service. The first was 'Wonderful Baby' in June 1992, followed by 'Spirit of Minot' in June 2015. (Robert Sullivan)

Ground crew servicing the General Electric M61A1 Vulcan 20mm rotary cannon during SAC's 1988 bombing and navigation exercise 'Proud Shield.' (Staff Sergeant Bob Simons)

project between the United States and the United Kingdom. Despite the interest, the project faced competition from submarine-launched ballistic missiles (SLBMs). In the face of a series of failures and the success of the SLBM programme, which would usher in the era of Lockheed's UGM-27 Polaris, the GAM-87 was wrapped up in December 1962.

The H would be fitted with new underwing pylons as part of the Improved Common Pylon (ICP) in the early 1960s, allowing it to carry a further 5,000lbs (2,267kg) per pylon. By the 1990s, the pylons were modified to carry slightly heavier loads, including the AGM-86. In 2021, it was recognized that there was a need to carry increasingly heavy air-dropped ordnance, including the 22,000lb (9,979kg) Massive Ordnance Air Burst (MOAB) bomb. To that end, the Air Force Materiel Command (AFMC) has recognized the need to upgrade the current pylon designs. The new pylons will appear within six years, quite possibly as part of the B-52 J/K upgrade.

A recent upgrade to the weapons carriage capacity of the H has been the introduction of Conventional Rotary Launchers (CRL) in November 2017. The CRL is explicitly designed to carry a selection of different conventional smart weapons or GPS-guided weapons, such as Lockheed Martin's stealth AGM-158C Long Range Anti-Ship Missile (LRASM) internally. The fitting of the CRL will allow the H to carry eight such weapons. By the beginning of the twenty-first century, the H could carry a staggering 70,000lbs (31,751kg) of ordnance.

Deliveries of the H began in early May 1961, with the 379th Bomb Wing at Wurtsmith AFB in Michigan being the first to receive the H. With the end of production in the autumn of 1962, after 102 airframes had been completed, production of the B-52 was considered complete. Sixty years later, a fantastic seventy-two B-52s, all H

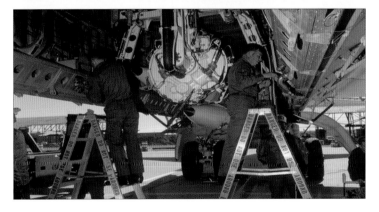

models, remain flying in squadron service across four Bomb Wings.

The redesigned wings of both the G and H models would experience greater stresses than those of previous models due to using aluminium alloys in their construction. Amid concerns around wing fatigue, and the loss of a G model belonging to the 4241st Strategic Wing due to a weakened wing, SAC placed a series of restrictions on G and H model B-52s in January 1961. This remained in place while a fix was sought, including substituting the wing box with a heavier gauge of aluminium. This project would come to be known as Engineering Change Proposal (ECP) 1050 in May 1961, and for $139 million, the project

A plumber's nightmare. The main landing-gear well of B-52H *Loko*, 96th Bomb Squadron, 2nd Bomb Wing, Barksdale AFB. (Robert Frola)

A B-52H nearing completion of its regeneration to active service in late 2020. It has spent ten years at the 309th Aerospace Maintenance and Regeneration Group's National-Level Airpower Reservoir located at Davis-Monthan AFB, Arizona. It will return to the 5th Bomb Wing at Minot AFB, North Dakota. (Ron Mullan)

Due to cracks found during a phase inspection, airmen from the 2nd Maintenance Squadron removed and replaced this B-52H's rudder. Before the fin can be lifted work is inspected to ensure quality assurance standards are met. (Senior Airman Micaiah Anthony)

ran from 1962 to 1964. With the exception of eighteen H models under construction at Wichita that received their modified wings, all aircraft were given their modifications during their routine Inspect and Repair as Necessary (IRAN) visits.

Serial production of the B-52 started in 1954 and finished in 1963, with Boeing producing 744 airframes. 1958 was its most productive year, with no fewer than 187 B-52s of three types leaving production lines. The final manufacturing figures for each model were A: three, B: fifty, C: thirty-five, D: 170, E: 100, F: eighty-nine, G: 193 and H: 102.

B-52J(K) – B-52 Commercial Engine Replacement Programme (CERP) Rapid Virtual Prototyping (RVP)

This was the most ambitious upgrade project to date for the B-52. It would see the eight venerable Pratt & Whitney TF33-P-3/103 turbofans replaced with the larger diameter Rolls Royce F130 (BR725) turbofans, which would allow the B-52 to maintain its four-pod, eight-engine appearance. The new engines would be sited higher and farther forward than their Pratt & Whitney predecessors. Other changes included the installation of a variant of the AN/APG-79 radar as used by the McDonnell Douglas F/A-18 Hornet, which saw the deletion of the under-nose blisters, returning to a clean nose reminiscent of the earlier B-52s. The forward-looking Electro-Optical Viewing System (EVS), which provided information to enable terrain avoidance and deliver battle assessment, would be removed, with some of those functions migrating to the new radar or a wing-mounted Litening (forward-looking infrared (FLIR) and laser designator) or Sniper (electro-optical targeting system) pods. Other upgrades include a new electrical power generation system, cockpit displays, and communications and navigation equipment. The refurbished aircraft will be designated B-52J during the transition period before becoming B-52K, becoming operational before the end of the 2020s, allowing the B-52 to continue flying until the 2050s.

Refining the design: Key Systems Upgrades

The B-52 was not intended, nor designed to see the length of service it has, yet it stands as an absolute testimony to the original Boeing design team as it prepares to be one of the first operational military aircraft to enter a century of service. As the B-52 developed, both as a strategic asset and an aeroplane, Boeing and other concerns, guided by the SAC and USAF, were quick to respond to the technological and service upgrades required. Some of those key changes, delivered over seventy years, have allowed Boeing and the USAF to deliver and field a weapons platform par excellence.

Air-Launched Cruise Missile Integration

Top: With the B-1 and B-2 being considered for retirement by the 2030s, the B-52 will have out-served the aircraft designed to replace it. (Sergeant Samuel Rogers)

Left: Ground crew perform maintenance on one of the Pratt & Whitney J57-P-43WB turbojets of a B-52G during Operation Desert Shield. (Chief Master Sergeant Don Sutherland)

The Air-Launched Cruise Missile (ALCM) was a weapon designed to overcome technological advances made by the Soviets in the 1970s whose air defences were becoming increasingly more efficient. An aeroplane the size of the B-52, despite the ADM-20 drone system, was still a good-sized target that could be taken on and defeated by relatively primitive air defences, as proven by the North Vietnamese. To that end, SAC returned to the proverbial drawing board to contemplate the future use of the B-52 as a weapons delivery platform. Their deliberations led them to the point where the ALCM could be launched beyond air defences' reach, preventing aircrews from facing the feared Soviet air defences. With

adopting the ALCM came new tactics, and the carrying aeroplane could now 'adopt a stand-off capacity as well as a shoot-and-penetrate capacity. Both would see the ALCMs launched safely in friendly skies, with the latter tactic seeing the carrying aeroplane moving on to attack secondary targets with gravity weapons.

Boeing would be awarded the contract for the ALCM, with their AGM-86B, which could carry both conventional and thermonuclear warheads, making it into front-line squadron service from December 1982. Ninety-eight Gs, with modified wing root fairings to help identify them as ALCM carriers, as per the agreements set in the Strategic Arms Limitation (SALT II)

Airmen attach an umbilical connector to a training AGM-86B ALCM during a B-52 load demonstration at Andersen AFB, Guam. (Senior Airman Benjamin Wiseman)

Six pylon-mounted AGM-86Bs are guided into position on a remotely controlled trolley under the port wing of a B-52G, identifiable by the engine nacelle cooling inlets. (Staff Sergeant Bob Simons)

arrangement, were equipped to carry the new AGM-86B. Ninety-six Hs would also be adapted, though unlike the G models they would be fitted with an internal Common Strategic Rotary Launcher (CSRL). This fitting would allow them to add a further eight missiles to the twelve already carried on underwing pylons, like the G.

Eventually, the USAF could call on 194 thus-equipped B-52s, putting the United States over its SALT limit of 1,320 deployable strategic nuclear delivery systems. The AGM-86, which had a speed of 560mph (901km/h) and a range over 1,500 miles (2,414km), would see service as a conventional missile in Iraq in 1990.

The many fears NATO had surrounding Soviet air defences would prove to be unfounded. On 28 May 1987, German teenager Mathias Rust landed a single-engine Reims Cessna F172P on Red Square after bypassing air defence, making a mockery of Soviet Air Defence Forces and Western intelligence estimates.

B-61 Mod 11 programme

The B-61 Mod 11 programme involved developing and testing a modified B-61 Silver Bullet thermonuclear gravity bomb on operational B-52s. Replacement of a strategic weapon was recommended by the 1993 Nuclear Posture Review and directed by Presidential Decision Review-30. The modifications to the B-61 Mod 7 strategic bomb, made by the Department of Energy, would allow the weapon system to accomplish the mission requirements of the replaced Mod 1 and 2 B-61s. Flight testing was carried out by the 419th Flight Test Squadron based at Edwards AFB, California, and certified that the modified weapon mass and physical properties were the same as the live Mod 7 device through the use of inert B-61s. At the same time,

When introduced in 1968, the 2K12 Kub (SA-6 Gainful) SAM missiles seen here at Batajnica airbase, Serbia, forced SAC to review its doctrine of unhindered high-level bombing. (Srđan Popović)

the AGM-130 air-to-ground guided missile integration on the B-52 was undertaken, and the programme was completed in 1997.

Big Belly

The Big Belly programme was undertaken due to combat experiences in Vietnam. The project increased the conventional weapon carriage capacity of 150 B-52Ds from twenty-seven weapons to eighty-four 500-lbs (227-kg) Mk82 general-purpose bombs, or forty-two 750-lbs (340kg) M117 demolition bombs. The project also saw the modification of the wing pylons, which allowed the carriage of a further twenty-four bombs of either type. This project increased the weapons payload to 60,000lbs (27,215kg). A further project, which ran from 1969 to 1971, would see some of the Ds further modified to carry aerial mines.

Big Four

As with all major projects, especially a new-generation aeroplane such as the B-52, there would always be changes in operational use that would necessitate occasional expensive fixes. An early and critical modification, also known as Modification 1000, was Big Four, initiated in 1959 to begin the first major upgrade of SAC's B-52 fleet, covering all models except the B. Big Four was designed to adapt the B-52 into becoming a correctly equipped low-level strike asset in response to the growing Soviet ICBM threat and the recently implemented dispersal programme. An additional boost to the project was that the Soviet air defences were, at the time, considered challenging to overcome; their low-level defences were operating at a far lower level of effectiveness. This project was deliberately aimed at exploiting this Achilles Heel. Except for the B, the remaining B-52 fleet could operate at 500ft (152m), easily operating in this loophole. The new offensive doctrine would also require structural changes and airframe strengthening programmes, with the C and D models being the most affected.

One of the first tasks carried out by the Oklahoma City Air Materiel Area (OCAMA)

based at Tinker AFB, Oklahoma, was to fit the Sperry AN/ALQ-27 Multiband Automatic Jamming and Deception System to 572 B-52s. SAC believed that the AN/ALQ-27 would give the B-52 an edge in its capacity to automatically counter ground-to-air and air-to-air missiles' airborne and ground fire control systems. It would also act as an early warning system and be capable of detecting the Soviet ground control interception radars. However, the cost of fitting the system fleet-wide proved prohibitive. It sat around $1 billion, meaning the Air Staff and OCAMA had to revise their plans. The AN/ALQ-27 was put aside, instead, a combination of quick reaction capability (QRC)/ECM equipment package was chosen. This was to be fitted to the H models then coming off Wichita production lines, before being retrofitted to the remaining B-52 fleet.

The cost of making any modifications was always expected to be high, and even with the removal of the AN/ALQ-27, the project's total expenditure of $313 million was nearly double the initial estimate of $192 million. Despite the increasing costs, exacerbated by differences between individual models that necessitated various solutions, SAC remained resolute in their commitment to maintaining the changes and ensuring their quality. One significant area of concern was the growing list of technical alterations needed

Right: The control panel of the National Cash Register Company's Computer, Altitude Vertical Velocity, AN/ASQ-38. (Estate of David P. Leising/ National Air and Space Museum)

Far right: Christi Blair and Cody Jack work on the B-52 Combat Network Communications Technology (CONECT) upgrade carried out at Tinker AFB, Oklahoma. (Marlin Zimmerman)

to make the B-52 suitable for low-level flights. Initial assessments had led the various teams involved to believe that the avionics upgrades could address the shift from high- to low-level operations. These improvements included enhancements to the Sperry-Rand MA-6A bombing navigation system, modification of the Doppler radar, and the addition of terrain clearance radar. The MA-6A would ultimately be replaced by the IBM AN/ASQ-48 by 1964. The avionic upgrades continued to be costly, with the modification of the National Cash Register Company's Computer, Altitude Vertical Velocity AN/ASQ-38, proving to be one of the more expensive upgrades for the model E and beyond. The next challenge facing the Big Four programme was the development of low-level radar. This proved to be a complex task, but by September 1963, these radars were in place. Another crucial addition was the incorporation of low-altitude altimeters and fittings for the AGM-28 air-launched cruise missile (ALCM).

The final avionics fit would see the Electronic Countermeasures (ECM) package implemented in several phases. Phase I involved an emergency modification that provided the essential ECM equipment required to counter Soviet air defences. Phase II was a project based on an ECM retrofit, utilizing components that were either equal in capacity to, or nearly as sophisticated as, those planned for Phase III. Phase III would see the B-52 equipped with the most advanced contemporary ECM equipment, rivaling the deleted AN/ALQ-27 Multiband Automatic Jamming and Deception System. This phase covered all B-52 models from H onwards, automatically fitted to enable low-level and all-weather flight.

Blue Band, Hard Shell, and Quickclip

The earlier B-52 models, from A to D, experienced fuel leaks due to Marman coupling failures that connected the fuel lines to each cell. Given the complexity of addressing this issue, which could impact nearly 180 aircraft, it was deemed more practical to distribute replacement CF-14 clamps to individual B-52 bases rather than transport individual aircraft back to Boeing. This project, known as Blue Band, was completed in September 1957. However, by the end of the year, despite the efficiency of installing the fix, the new clamps were found to be susceptible to failure. This realization led to the development of another fix known as Hard Shell.

Boeing and the USAF examined the issues and believed they had found a solution by developing a stainless-steel clamp known as CF-17s. The project was completed by January 1958, but the problem persisted. A modified clamp called the CF-17A, featuring strengthened latch pins, was introduced as a quick fix, but neither Boeing nor the USAF were satisfied. This led to a new set of flight restrictions and an ongoing quest for a solution.

The Quickclip project aimed to address the fuel line issues and was extended to include the E and some F model B-52s. The installation of safety straps around the CF-17A clamps resolved the issue of leaking clamps. The refit was completed by the summer of 1958 and was considered successful. The latest F models leaving Seattle and Wichita were equipped with the new safety straps during production.

Combat Network Communications Technology (CONECT)

Commencing in 2005, the Combat Network Communications Technology (CONECT) programme represented the first significant communications upgrade for the B-52 since the 1960s. Implemented as part of the Programmed Depot Maintenance rotation at Tinker AFB, Oklahoma, all seventy-six H models underwent the CONECT upgrade. Led by Boeing, the CONECT programme transformed the B-52 by replacing its analogue systems with a digital-based system. Crews were provided with keyboards and trackballs and could upload mission data via a thumb drive.

CONECT could be updated in real-time through machine-to-machine digital transmission while the aircraft was in flight, allowing for mission redirection as the strategic and tactical situation changed. This system eliminated the potential for input errors, crucial for the effective use of innovative weapon systems. The CONECT system also eliminated the need for complex pre-flight mission design, which could become outdated by the time of execution.

All information was conveyed to crews via LCD screens running on Windows software, reducing training costs and providing the crew with more time to complete reports during flight. CONECT was intentionally designed to be adaptable, with its software capable of accommodating new avionics and weapon systems as needed.

The 565th Aircraft Maintenance Squadron completed the programme, incorporating the 7,000-hour installation into the aircraft's programmed maintenance. The project was finalized in 2016 and will continue to be a vital component of the remaining B-52 aircraft as they are developed into the J and K models.

Conventional Enhancement Modification (CEM)

The Conventional Enhancement Modification (CEM), which began in 1994, enabled the H model to carry guided GBU 31/32 Joint Direct Attack Munitions (JDAM), the AGM-154 Joint Standoff Weapon (JSOW), and other Global Positioning System (GPS)-directed weapon systems. To facilitate this, the CEM upgrade included the GPS navigation receiver and a Rockwell-Collins AN/ARC-210 UHF/VHF AM/FM Communications system, which featured secure voice encryption and anti-jam capabilities.

This system worked alongside the existing Rockwell-Collins AN/ARC-171(V) UHF Satellite Communications Radio Set, providing the aircraft access to the United States military satellite communications system. This allowed the B-52 to communicate from anywhere in the world. In addition to the AN/ARC-210, the H model was equipped with an AN/AS-3858 / AN/AAR-85T(T) Miniature Receive Terminal (MRT), a five-channel LF/VLF receiver.

Also included was the MIL-STD 1760 electrical interconnection system to support the use of JDAM and JSOW, which would

Loading a Joint Direct Attack Munitions (JDAM) onto the B-52H weapons pylon during Operation Inherent Resolve, which aimed to eliminate the Da'esh (ISIS) threat in South West Asia. (Senior Airman Miles Wilson)

be externally carried on the wing pylons. In 2015, this capability was supplemented by a Conventional Rotary Launcher, enabling the internal carriage of smart munitions such as JDAM and JSOW. The installation of the underwing Heavy Stores Adapter Beam (HSAB) on each wing store's pylon allowed the carriage of stores incompatible with the original pylon system due to their size.

ECM Support Improvement Plan (SIP)

By the late 1990s, the three major defensive ECM systems of the B-52, the AN/ALQ-172, AN/ALQ-155, and AN/ALR-20, required upgrades or replacement due to performance, reliability, and compatability issues. There was also an enhancement requirement for the other defensive systems on the remaining B-52s to ensure the ECM suite remained operationally viable.

Between October 1996 and March 1997, it was discovered that the B-52's ECM suite had become the leading cause of the Air Combat Command's B-52 bomber wings not meeting their Mission Capable (MC) rate standards. Clearly, the B-52's three major defensive systems all needed upgrades or replacement. During these six months, these three systems combined to produce a six-month Mission Incapable (MICAP) driver rate for the B-52 fleet of more than 43,000 hours. At the same time, ECM operators discovered that readiness spare packages (RSP) kits had been depleted of several critical system line replaceable units (LRU), significantly impacting the operational readiness of the entire H model fleet.

In March 1997, USAF and Boeing management at Tinker AFB, Oklahoma, implemented an ECM Support Improvement Plan (SIP). The SIP sought to improve the ECM MICAP rate and RSP fill rates to acceptable levels. As a result, they had eliminated MICAPs by April 1997 and filled RSP kits to the Independent Kit Level by May 1997, improving H model service operability.

ECP1050

Engineering Change Proposal (ECP) 1050 was an Inspect and Repair as Necessary

A CRL loaded with GBU 31/32 Joint Direct Attack Munitions (JDAM) is readied at Al Udeid Air Base, Qatar, for its next mission against targets in Afghanistan. (Staff Sergeant Patrick Evenson)

AGM-69A Short-Range Attack Missile (SRAM) with their rotary launcher are downloaded during Exercise Global Shield, 1984. (Technical Sergeant Boyd Belcher)

B-52H 60-053 from the 2d Bomb Wing, Barksdale AFB, Louisiana, prepares for a local training mission with EVS nose sensors ready for use. Sadly, 60-053 went down off the coast of Guam on 21 July 2008, with the loss of all six crew members. (Technical Sergeant Robert Horstman)

(IRAN) depot tasking that covered remedial work on the wing structure of the G and H models. The ECP ran from February 1962 to September 1964 and included replacing the wing box beam with a new unit featuring thicker aluminium and replacing the titanium taper lock fasteners with steel fasteners. Further strengthening was achieved by adding extra brackets and clamps to the wings' skins, as well as additional panel stiffeners. Another improvement involved applying a new protective coating to the internal wing fuel tanks. Almost all of the final eighteen H models received their ECP 1050 modifications during their routine IRAN visits.

ECP2126

Engineering Change Proposal (ECP) 2126 focused on enabling 270 G and H models to carry and launch the AGM-69A Short-Range Attack Missile (SRAM). The nuclear-capable SRAM could be fitted to modified wing pylons and a rotary bomb bay launcher, along with the necessary avionic updates. The upgrades allowed the B-52s to carry twelve missiles on the pylons and eight on the internal rotary bomb bay launcher. The first completed B-52, a G model belonging to the 42nd Bomb Wing based at Loring AFB, Maine, was finished in March 1972 and was fully operational by August of the same year.

Due to the size and complexity of the modification, two locations were responsible for the upgrades. Oklahoma Air Materiel Area handled the G models, while San Antonio Air Materiel Area at Kelly AFB in Texas managed the H models.

Electro-Optical Viewing System (EVS)

The AN/ASQ-151 EVS package has its roots in a local modification carried out by Boeing's Chief of Flight Test, Jack Funk, in the mid-1960s. Funk had a Sony television camera installed in the tail of the B-52 to monitor tests, and, despite its relative crudeness, the use of the camera was picked up by the then USAF liaison officer, Colonel Rick Hudlow. Hudlow's imagination was sparked, and he mentioned Funk's modification to representatives in SAC, who, in turn, issued a requirement to examine the possibilities of using visual sensors on the B-52.

In 1965, the requirement to explore visual sensors became an SAC-sponsored project, looking at using sensors to improve damage assessment and strike capacity. The project would also examine how sensors could support existing terrain-avoidance equipment. The intent was to fit the G and H models with the cameras and associated systems. After five years of testing, a production order was placed.

Between 1971 and 1976, 270 B-52s received the AN/ASQ-151 EVS package. The package was made up of the steerable Westinghouse AN/AVQ-22 Low-Light TV

Electro-Optical Viewing System (LLL-TV) and the Hughes AN/AAQ-6 forward-looking infra-red (FLIR) Electro-Optical Viewing System. Both systems would be placed under the aircraft, giving B-52s with this particular fit a unique appearance. Operator display screens, a servo control unit, and a symbol signal generator would back up the two systems.

The screen would provide the viewers with information that included an overload terrain avoidance profile trace from either the LLL-TV or FLIR and height readings from the radar altimeter. Other information included time-to-go before weapon release and operating symbology, including artificial horizon and indicated airspeed.

Engineering Sustainment Programme (ESP)

The Engineering Sustainment Programme (ESP) was a ten-year engineering programme awarded to Boeing in June 2009. The central premise of the programme was for Boeing to provide engineering and technical support services for the remaining H models and their components, as well as support and test equipment, alongside the provision of a system integration laboratory. Boeing also installed an extremely high-frequency (EHF) system enabling the aircraft to exchange data with the ground station from ground, air, and space platforms and upgraded the communications system of the B-52H bomber aircraft.

Hi-Stress

The Hi-Stress project was a three-phase structural fix programme running alongside the Big Four project. Starting in 1960, the first phase sought to strengthen the fuselage bulkheads and aileron bay areas and reinforce the boost pump panels and wing foot splice plates of those B-52s nearing 2,000 hours of flight time. Phase Two was more extensive in its remit and was applied to those airframes approaching 2,500 hours of flight time. The B-52s covered by this phase would see the reinforcement of various wing areas, including upper wing splices, fuel probe access doors, and portions of the lower fuselage bulkhead.

The final phase, three, was treated as an Inspect and Repair as Necessary (IRAN) tasking focusing on early B-52s and dealt with wing fractures. This phase was carried out by approved contractors, who were guided by specialist teams from the Oklahoma City and San Antonio Air Materiel Areas.

Hot Fan

This programme was established to increase the engine reliability of the Pratt & Whitney TF33 early within its service with the H fleet as well as eliminate the possibility of failure before 600 hours of operation. Led and delivered by Oklahoma City Air Material Area (OCAMA), Hot Fan would cover throttle issues, flame-outs,

Technicians remove the EVS sensor cowling during maintenance on a B-52H during Exercise Gallant Eagle, 1982. (Staff Sergeant Bill Thompson)

excessive oil consumption, turbine blade failure, and inlet case cracks. Hot Fan was surprisingly cheap for such a broad remit, costing the taxpayer £15 million.

Hot Fan started in mid-1962, but the Cuban Missile Crisis would stall the project as the entire B-52 fleet was put on standby. The programme was resumed the following January and was completed in late 1964, after 894 engines had been overhauled.

Crew chiefs re-install a B-52H leading edge fairing; it allows ground crew access to all fuel lines, hydraulic lines, electrical wires and cables running from the wing to the cockpit. (Airman 1st Class Mozer Da Cunha)

The AGM-158 JASSM (Joint Air-to-Surface Standoff Missile) is a low-observable standoff cruise missile whose development began in 1995, but problems during testing delayed its introduction into service until 2009. (Robert Frola)

Sam Denison, of the 49th Test and Evaluation Squadron at Barksdale AFB, Louisiana, installs IRIS into a B-52. (Senior Airman Jonathan Ramos)

An early B-52 with a mounted AGM-28 Hound Dog.
(National Museum of the US Air Force)

Internal Weapons Bay Upgrade (IWBU)

Military Standard 1760 Internal Weapons Bay Upgrade (IWBU) started in September 2013, was designed to allow the B-52 to carry up to eight advanced precision-guided Joint Direct Attack Munitions (JDAM) internally. A contract for Engineering and Manufacturing Development was awarded to Boeing to develop and produce six IWBU by April 2016, with additional units to follow an Air Force post-installation review.

To achieve this, Boeing designed the IWBU by simply rewiring the existing B-52 launcher into a bomb bay fitted with a Common Rotary Launcher. The rewiring equipped the B-52 with a storage management overlay (SMO) software interface. Weapons systems covered under this fit include the Lockheed Martin AGM-158B Joint Air-to-Surface Standoff Missile – Extended Range (JASSM-ER) and the Raytheon Missile Systems ADM-160 MALD (Miniature Air-Launched Decoy). The new wiring has also been designed to be adapted to manage future weapon payloads.

The new system complements the twelve munitions the B-52 can already carry on its exterior weapons pylons; this modification allows the B-52 to carry twenty such weapon systems.

IRIS

The IRIS beyond-line-of-sight (BLOS) communication system will replace the Global Iridium Bomber Set (GLIBS) that has been in service since 2017, providing complete global coverage by leveraging the Low Earth Orbit (LEO) Iridium NEXT satellite constellation. IRIS is an Air Force Global Strike Command (AFGSC) programme that will integrate the B-52 fleet into the greater Joint All-Domain Command and Control system after successful trials in the summer of 2022.

Jolly Well

Jolly Well was the project name for the bomb and navigation systems upgrade and addressed outstanding avionics issues. This saw the IBM AN/ASQ-38 Computer, Altitude Vertical Velocity originally fitted to the E and F models, experience a series of upgrades. The project was completed in 1964 and affected 480 B-52s. The fundamental changes were the improvements, including low-level terrain avoidance and the replacement of the terrain computer.

Malfunction Detection and Recording

Malfunction Detection and Recording (MADREC) was a modification applied to the entire B-52 fleet after a capacity requirement was made in 1961. The MADREC project was designed to detect avionics and weapons computer system failures. It was essential in monitoring the AGM-52 Hound Dog air-launched cruise missile (ALCM). The project was carried out in two phases: the first covers models B to

A gunner programmes a console at his station on a B-52H. (CPT Rosell)

D and was completed by the summer of 1963. The second phase, which covered the E model, was completed by 1965.

Offensive Avionics System (OAS)

The AN/ASQ-176 Offensive Avionics System (OAS) was designed to replace the IBM/Raytheon AN/ASQ-38 Bombing/Navigation System fitted to the G and H models. The AN/ASQ-38 had not aged well, suffering operational setbacks, including malfunctions. In 1975, the USAF finally sought to remove these problems. The use of digital technology by the OAS would be extensive, which led to a programme of suitability testing starting in September 1980.

The first and most crucial step was to check weapons integration with the OAS, and in June 1981, it was used to successfully launch an AGM-69 Short-Range Attack Missile (SRAM). The design of the OAS was guided by a military standard that defines the mechanical, electrical, and operating characteristics of a serial data communication bus for the US Department of Defense, known as the Mil-Std-1553A. This saw the introduction of new controls, displays, a radar altimeter, and an inertial navigation system, all hardened against post-nuclear detonation electromagnetic pulse (EMP). It also introduced an attitude heading reference system, missile interface units, and an update to the primary attack radar. The OAS was a noticeable improvement on the AN/ASQ-38 and was designed for low-level use. The OAS programme was completed by the mid-1980s for £1.66 billion.

Pacer Plank

Approved in 1972, Pacer Plank was a life extension project covering the D model. It was led by Boeing under an Engineering Change Proposal (ECP) known as ECP1581.

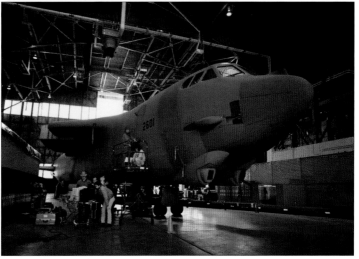

Carried out at the Wichita facility, the ECP saw that the lower wing was redesigned. New alloys were used to re-skin the reworked surfaces. Other changes on the wing included the redesign and replacement of the wing centre panel and the incorporation of new upper longerons. The fuselage also received some attention by installing a new bulkhead in the forward fuselage and replacing some fuselage side skins. The Pacer Plank project was completed in 1977.

Pave Mint/Have Exit

Starting in 1981, the Pave Mint/Have Exit project evolved into the Rivet Ace Electronic Counter Measures (ECM) upgrade project. It featured the use of an International Telegraph and Telephone (IT&T) Avionics (ITTAV) AN/ALQ-172 (V)1 Countermeasures System (CMS) radar warning system in the G model. The AN/ALQ-172 used the antennas previously used by the AN/ALQ-117 Active Countermeasures Set. The AN/ALQ-117 noise/deception jamming system utilized twin tail-mounted sensors to detect

A team of researchers from the Non-destructive Evaluation Sciences Branch (NESB) performs tests with the Magneto-Optical Imager (MOI) on the fuselage of a B-52 aircraft as part of NASA's Airframe Structural Integrity Programme (NASIP). Note the two-tone grey camouflage. (Defense Visual Information Distribution Service)

Right: A B-52H shortly after the explosive charges have been detonated on the engines in preparation for a MITO exercise at Barksdale AFB, Louisiana. (Staff Sgt. Sean Martin)

Below: A diagram giving the location of all the avionics found on a 2000 B-52H. (Unknown)

Bottom: Ground crew load an ATM-84A onto a B-52G wing pylon during a squadron training exercise. (Chief Master Sergeant Don Sutherland)

radar-directed missiles and guns. The project was deemed completed by 1986 on all G models.

The H models were given the AN/ALQ-172 (V)2 system that featured an electronically steerable phased array and was declared operational in 1988. The system proved unreliable; high maintenance costs led to Engineering Change Proposal (ECP) 93, a modification programme designed to improve these systems' memory and processing capability. In 1997, because of ECP93, an additional AN/ALQ-172 system was deemed appropriate to provide complete threat protection.

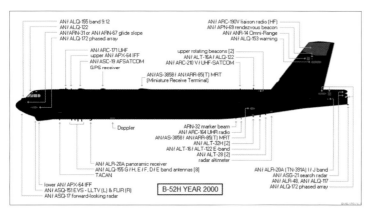

Quick Start

Quick Start was the final programme by SAC to enable its B-52s to take off in the fastest time possible. Emulating an earlier programme that took place between 1963 and 1964, Quick Start was applied to G and H models with cartridge starters added to each engine. This allowed simultaneous ignition of all eight engines, reducing the time to take off considerably. Not all engines needed the modification as some had been previously modified at the start of SAC's dispersal programme, which saw operational B-52s fitted with two cartridge starters. Not only did the installation of the cartridge starters improve the reaction time, but it also allowed B-52s to operate from remote sites, not necessarily equipped with the specialist ground support equipment needed. This process is called a Cart Start, allowing aircraft to perform a Minimum Interval Takeoff (MITO).

Rapid Eight

The G models that were not converted as cruise missile carriers underwent a series of modifications to improve conventional bombing and were fitted with a new Integrated Conventional Stores Management System (ICSMS). These B-52s also received an upgrade of their underwing pylons that could now carry larger payloads than the previously fitted pylons. Thirty Gs were modified to carry up to twelve AGM-84 Harpoon anti-ship missiles each. At the same time, a further twelve were equipped to carry the AGM-142 Have Nap stand-off air-to-ground missile. With the retirement of the G models in 1994, a programme was initiated to ensure the B-52Hs could carry and use the AGM-84 and AGM-142. Subsequently, four Hs were modified under the Rapid Eight programme.

Rivet Ace

Engineering Change Proposal (ECP) 2519, started in December 1971, also known as the Phase VI Electronic Countermeasures (ECM) Defensive Avionics Systems, and was given the project name Rivet Ace. The project covered the G and H models, and the few visible changes saw the extreme rear of the fuselage extended by 40in (1,016mm) to help accommodate new equipment, as well as various antennas and blisters. Given the complexity of Rivet Ace, the first few years of the project focused on design and development to ensure the new system was as operationally capable as possible. The modification project began once the designs had been finessed and configurations had been agreed on.

The new equipment fit was comprehensive and consisted of the Tasker Inc AN/ALR-20A Panoramic Countermeasures Radar Warning Receiver; the Litton (Dalmo Victor) AN/ALR-46 (V) Digital Warning Receiver; the ITT AN/ALQ-117 Active Countermeasures Set; the Motorola AN/ALQ-122 False Target Generator, also referred to as Smart Noise Operation Equipment; the Hallicrafters AN/ALT-28 noise jammer; the Northrop Grumman (Westinghouse) AN/ALQ-153 Active Missile Approach Warning System; the Northrop AN/ALT-32H and AN/ALT-32L high-and-low band communications jammers; and the Hallicrafters/Sperry AN/ALT-16A D-Band Noise Barrage Jammer. Alongside this remarkable upgrade sat twelve AN/ALE-20 infra-red flare dispensers, which carried 192 flares and eight Lundy AN/ALE-24 chaff dispensers capable of deploying 1,125 bundles. The Rivet Ace project was completed in the late 1980s and was further refined under the Pave Mint programme from September 1986.

Rivet Rambler

The Rivet Rambler project was designed to enhance the Electronic Warfare capability of the D models, with installation taking place between 1967 and 1969. Known as Phase V, Rivet Rambler would later be extended to cover those G models assigned to conventional warfare missions in Southeast Asia. The fit itself consisted of a General Electric AN/ALR-18 Threat Detection Receiver; a Tasker Inc AN/ALR-20 Panoramic Countermeasures Radar Warning Receiver; an Itek AN/APR-25 S/X/C-Band Radar Detection and Homing Set; four General Electric AN/ALT-6B Multi-Band Jammers, featuring Magnetron plugins for L/S/X bands or General Electric/Burroughs/ Litton AN/ALT-22 Continuous Wave Jamming Transmitters. Also fitted were two Hallicrafters/Sperry AN/ALT-16 D-Band Noise Barrage Jammers; two Northrop AN/ALT-32H and AN/ALT-32L high-and-low band communications jammers; and six AN/ALE-20 infra-red flare dispensers which carried 192 flares and eight Lundy AN/ALE-24 chaff dispensers capable of deploying 1,125 bundles.

The G models which received this fit were also given a Boeing AN/ALE-25 Decoy Rocket Pod fitted with Tracor ADR-8A

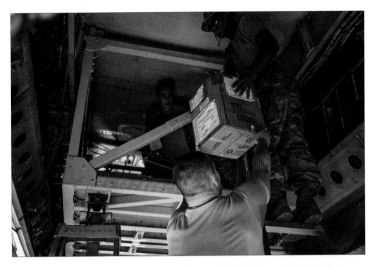

Airmen unload a B-52's On-Board Cargo System (BOCS) after an Agile Combat Employment Exercise whose purpose is to move aircraft to networks of small, dispersed locations for a range of tactical and strategic reasons. (Airman Nicole Ledbetter)

unguided electronic countermeasures rockets. The twenty-shot AN/ALE-25 were mounted on pylons under the wings of the Gs but were later removed in September 1970 as part of the Rivet Ace project and replaced by the corresponding electronic warfare suite. Several Guam-based Gs were fitted with the Northrop Grumman (Westinghouse) AN/ALQ-119 S/X/C-Band Noise/Deception Jamming Pods instead of the AN/ALE-25 during Operation Linebacker in 1972.

Sea Fish and Giant Fish

Based at Castle AFB, California, at least four F models were provided with a high-altitude air-sampling pod to capture atmospheric radiation samples in the mid-1950s. To gather the samples, a specialist pod was installed in the forward area of the internal weapons bay and operated from the gunner's workstation by specialist airmen. The pod contained three filter changers for particle samples, two static stations used as a reference during data analysis, and eight gaseous sampling 'balls'. Each pod's installation and set-up took eight hours, with two B-52s taking off as the others landed. The aim was to

A far cry from the early systems, the Weapons Systems Officer (WSO) of this B-52G programmes his mission via an onboard computer during the 1987 SAC Proud Shield bombing competition. (Master Sergeant Locati)

The Soviet equivalent of the B-52 was the Tupolev TU-95, which entered service in 1956. The TU-95 would deliver the fifty Megaton Tsar Bomba, the largest yield special weapon ever produced. (Russian Ministry of Defence)

The abandoned town of Pripyat and the Chernobyl sarcophagus bear witness to the disaster that befell the area in the early hours of 26 April 1986. (Konung Yaropolk)

provide scientific data to enable civilian and military engineers and scientists with reliable data from Soviet nuclear testing. The role was then taken over by the Boeing WC-135 weather reconnaissance aircraft in the 1960s. Still, there were occasions when the B-52s were required to fill the gaps in operational capacity.

With the withdrawal from service of the F model in the early 1970s, two H models were modified to carry the high-altitude air sampling pod in a programme known as Giant Fish. Like Sea Fish, the project's objective was to provide H models with the ability to capture air samples in the event of possible radiation releases. These were later replaced by two other H models that flew out of Carswell AFB, Texas. One of its most critical missions was to capture samples of the Chernobyl reactor explosion in 1986, with thirteen sorties in total being flown.

One aeroplane would always remain on standby, in case a satellite should fall to earth, to measure any residual radiation; interestingly, this Quick Reaction Aircraft would carry the full ammunition load for the rear M61 20mm cannon. These B-52s would operate from several locations, including Hawaii, often working with allied

air partners, including the Royal Air Force, to compare standards and results.

By the early 1990s, Carswell AFB was closed due to the end of the Cold War, and the force was split between Fairchild AFB, Washington, and Minot AFB before being stood down not long after.

Senior Bowl

Project Senior Bowl was a Central Intelligence Agency (CIA)-led project using the forerunner to Lockheed's SR-71 Blackbird, the twin-seat M-21, a drone-carrying variant of the single-seat A-12 high-altitude strategic reconnaissance aeroplane. The intent had been for the M-21 to fly missions solely for the CIA equipped with Lockheed's D-21 unmanned reconnaissance drone. On 30 July 1966, an M-21 was lost following an attempt to launch a D-21 drone. Lockheed's Kelly Johnson, the famous Skunk Works team leader, stopped all further developments of the M-21 and D-21 pairing, leading to a B-52H being chosen to act as a mothership, following in the footsteps of Fortress predecessors.

During the spring of 1967, Tinker-based Oklahoma Air Materiel Area undertook the necessary work to allow the B-52 to carry two D-21s, known as D-21Bs, on underwing pylons. Meanwhile, the Burbeck-based Skunk Works worked on the D-21 to enable it to be fitted to the pylons that generally carry the AGM-28. Once mounted, the B-52 mothership would launch the D-21Bs via a jettisonable booster rocket that accelerated the drone until its internal Marquardt RJ43-MA-20S4 ramjet ignited safely from the B-52.

Flying from Beale AFB, California, between April 1968 and October 1971, the H, belonging to the 4200th Support Squadron, would depart for Anderson AFB in Guam under darkness. Once it arrived at Anderson AFB, it would be prepared for operational sorties. It is believed only five missions, possibly over China to monitor China's nuclear weapons programme, were flown during this period.

A Barksdale AFB B-52H crew from 96th Bomb Squadron prepare to leave RAF Fairford, England, a well-established forward operating location for B-52s. (Staff Sergeant James Cason)

A B-52H carrying a D-21 reconnaissance drone with rocket booster, takes on fuel. (USAF)

South Bay

The South Bay project was designed to increase the bomb load capacity of twenty-eight F models. The project started in June 1964 and saw the earmarked B-52s receive modified wing pylons capable of carrying a further twenty-four 750lbs (340kg) M117 free-fall demolition bombs. The project was completed in October of the same year, with the adapted B-52s later undertaking combat operations in Vietnam.

Sun Bath

Sun Bath could be considered the follow-on project to South Bay, this time covering the upgrade of forty-six F models between June and July 1965. The then Defence Secretary Robert McNamara led the project with Oklahoma City Air Materiel Area drawing resources from the war reserve and Tactical Air Command. Like their predecessors, the Sun Bath B-52s would see operational service in Vietnam.

Strategic Radar Modification

In 1985, the Strategic Radar Modification replaced the AN/ASQ-176 Offensive Avionics System with the Northrop Grumman (Norden) AN/APQ-156 J-Band Navigation & Attack Radar. The AN/ASQ-176 consisted of a Northrop Grumman strategic radar; Honeywell radar altimeter; Smiths attitude heading and reference system; Tercom terrain comparison, Teledyne Ryan Doppler navigation radar; Honeywell AN/ASN-131 inertial navigation system; and IBM/Raytheon AN/ASQ-38 bombing and navigation system. Given the scale of the modification, it was understandably complex, with the fitting and replacement of numerous controls, displays, antenna units and radar processors.

Applied to all in-service B-52H and some B-52G models, the Strategic Radar Modification also saw the installation of new software to enhance targeting capacity and ease the not insignificant workload of the navigator/bombardier.

Sunflower

Project Sunflower would be the first of many large-scale upgrades the B-52 would experience throughout its service. From the summer of 1956 to December 1957, the programme aimed to upgrade seven early production Bs used for flight development and engineering feedback. This required almost 150 kits, installed to a configuration that closely matched the C model. Once completed, the seven Bs were assigned to squadron service.

Tee Town

By the late 1950s, Soviet air defences rapidly improved as technology became

A Lockheed D-21B and trolley at the National Museum of the United States Air Force (USAF)

more sophisticated. These developments left the SACs bomber fleet vulnerable to inception and attack from increasingly advanced fighters, radars, and surface-to-air missiles throughout the Soviet Union. Given that the SAC could draw on an impressive arsenal of aircraft, including the new B-52, it was imperative to fit the B-52 with a comprehensive and effective electronic countermeasures suite and a dedicated electronic warfare officer to operate the suite.

A project, subsequently named Tee Town, was designed to meet this need and was carried out between 1958 and 1959 with the assistance of Douglas Aircraft's Tulsa Division. Tee Town consisted of two 14ft (4.6m) pods mounted on cantilevered pylons attached to the bomb bay doors. Each pod carried four General Electric AN/ALT-6B Multi-Band jammers on the lower half of the pod and was covered by a fibreglass dielectric fairing. To cool the AN/ALT-6Bs, ram air was ducted around each unit, while upgraded electrical generators were provided to handle the increased electrical demand. Although only 120 pods were built, Tee Town was unique as it led to the world's first production electronic warfare jamming pod specifically designed for high-speed aircraft.

B-52H Specifications

Type: Heavy Bomber (introduced into service 1961)

Crew: Five: Aircraft commander, pilot, radar navigator, navigator and electronic warfare officer.

Engine: Eight Pratt & Whitney TF33-P-3/103 turbofans, with 17,000lbs (7,710kg) thrust per engine.

Performance:
Max Speed – 632mph (1,017kmh) maximum at 23,800ft (7,254m); cruising speed 525mph (845km/h)
Service Ceiling – 47,000ft (14,326m)
Combat radius with 10,000lbs (4,540kg) bomb load: 4,825mi (7,765km), Ferry range 10,145 miles (16,327km)

Weight:
Empty – 185,000lbs (83,250kg)
Max. Take-off weight – 488,000lbs (219,600kg)

Dimensions:
Span – 185ft (56m)
Length – 160ft 10.9in (48.7m)
Height – 40 ft 8in (12.19m)
Wing Area – 4,000ft² (311.6m²)

Armament: Approximately 70,000lbs (31,500kg) mixed ordnance – bombs, smart weapons, mines and missiles. Can be modified to carry air-launched cruise missiles (ALCM).

Total Produced: 102

In Service and In Action

B-52H of the 340th Weapons Squadron at Barksdale AFB, Louisiana, takes off during a US Air Force Weapons School Integration exercise at Nellis AFB, Nevada, 18 November 2021. (USAF/William R. Lewis)

The B-52 was operated solely by the United States, with the United States Air Force (USAF) flying most of the 744 aircraft built. Two B-52s were flown by the National Aeronautics and Space Administration (NASA) as motherships for scientific research, carrying on a tradition established by early Boeing bombers. The B-52 entered service during increased political and military uncertainty, with the Soviets developing a fearsome nuclear arsenal. Its arrival would see the USAF adapt its defensive doctrine with the re-introduction of the dispersal principle, designed to protect its precious B-52 fleet.

LeMay saw the B-52 and its crews as the elite of the SAC, with all involved, from service personnel to their families, given the best accommodation, services, food, and training. The B-52 was now a critical element of Operation Chrome Dome, which placed a nuclear-armed B-52 on continuous airborne alert around the continent of North America. Operation Chrome Dome provided the Americans with a rapid first-strike or retaliation capability should an attack against American targets by Soviet nuclear weapons occur. For eight years the B-52 crept along the edges of Soviet territory and its sphere of influence before being stood down. Despite not

The original 1964 Chrome Dome Mission Map from Sheppard AFB, Texas. (USAF Air Force Historical Research Agency)

deploying nuclear weapons, the B-52 force had lost several aircraft due to accidents, often due to refuelling manoeuvres. 1968 saw Operation Chrome Dome end as more advanced missile systems replaced the B-52.

SAC was now keen to utilize the conventional capabilities of the B-52, which had established itself as a reliable and hardy aeroplane. The B-52 had been flying in the skies of Southeast Asia, striking at North Vietnamese targets in Vietnam, Laos, and Cambodia since the mid-1960s. Although not involved in Operation Rolling Thunder, which ran from March 1965 to November 1968, the B-52 found its niche in the conventional Operation Arc Light operations, which began on 18 June 1965. B-52D, F, and G models flying from Guam

Crew chiefs from the 20th Aircraft Maintenance Unit perform a post-flight inspection on a B-52H during a Quick Regeneration Exercise at Barksdale AFB, Louisiana, February 2017. (Senior Airman Mozer O. Da Cunha)

and Thailand participated in Operation Arc Light. All would have their white, anti-flash underbellies repainted black to reduce visibility from the ground, with wrap-around camouflage soon following. When the mission ceased on 15 August 1973, the B-52s had flown 126,615 combat sorties. They lost thirty-one B-52s, eighteen to North Vietnamese defences and the remainder to operational losses.

The B-52 would also see action in Operation Linebacker and Operation Linebacker II, that took place in 1972. Operation Linebacker ran from 9 May to 23 October 1972. It focused on stopping or at least disrupting the transportation of North Vietnamese People's Army of Vietnam (PAVN) supplies and materials for the Nguyen Hue Offensive. Operation Linebacker II ran from 18–29 December, 1972, and focused on military and industrial targets in the Northern Vietnamese cities of Hanoi and Haiphong. By the time the Americans withdrew from Vietnam in March 1973, the B-52 had been developed to carry a staggering 60,000lbs (27,216kg) bomb load.

The Cold War continued, and the B-52 continued to be flown, albeit in decreasing numbers, as part of SAC's mission, acting as a conventional air deterrent with numerous weapons and avionics system upgrades taking place. The end of the Cold War saw the gradual reduction of conventional and nuclear forces across the globe, which had begun with the 1991 START I (Strategic Arms Reduction Treaty), sped up. With the gradual slimming down of the B-52 fleet, the USAF's long-term gaze was firmly fixed on ensuring the long-term future of the H model. The remaining previous models were retired, scrapped, or cocooned, despite

the challenges the West now faced in the uncertain post-Soviet world, especially the Middle East, where Operation Desert Storm and Desert Shield had recently finished. On 1 June 1992, Strategic Air Command was replaced by the United States Strategic Command (USSTRATCOM) and disbanded the same day, its mission complete.

By the end of the twentieth century, the B-52 had become a key symbol of strategic American military and political power. The War on Terror, sparked by the attacks on the World Trade Centre in 2001, saw the B-52 in action once more in the skies over Afghanistan and Iraq. Today, regular deployments are made to reassure both allies and adversaries that the B-52 Stratofortress remains a formidable weapon, capable of rapid deployment at a moment's notice.

A US Air Force B-52 bomber carrying a dozen 750-pound bombs under each wing and twenty-seven bombs inside the aircraft takes off from the US base in Guam to head for a strike against Viet Cong targets in South Vietnam during the Vietnam War, Guam. (Photo by Hulton Archive/Getty Images)

Stratofortress Variants

The North American X-15A-2 being carried by the NASA NB-52B *Balls 8* mothership, note the cut-out section of the wing. (USAF)

As with its predecessors, Boeing had created an almost perfect foundation in the B-52. It would be the subject of numerous technological improvements as the use of the aeroplane was refined and defined by experience, strategic considerations, and political events. With unintentional longevity achieved by the now almost legendary Boeing robustness, the B-52 would be pushed and pulled in ways the original design team had not imagined. While its wing and basic fuselage would see little significant changes, those that did occur gave the end user a weapon of such flexibility that it would be impossible to replace. Boeing had created the last word in a strategic bomber.

Those variants produced were mainly systems upgrades, which on the surface look inconsequential but were essential in the United States being able to continue its long-reach and research operations.

NB-52A and NB-52B *Balls 8*

The origins of the NB-52 motherships' can be traced back to mid-1957 when NASA directed North American Aviation (NAA) to change the captive-carry and launch mothership for their ongoing rocket-plane programme from Convairs B-36, the largest mass-produced piston-engine aircraft ever built, to Boeing's B-52. The main driver of NASA's insistence for change was the imminent B-36 retirement. It was realized that the B-36 would be phased out of service just as NAA's last project, the X-15 series of aircraft, was to begin flight trials. Perhaps previous positive experiences with the B-29 and B-50 mothership influenced the NASA decisions, aided partly by the realization that B-36 service support by Convair and the USAF would quickly disappear with the aeroplane's retirement.

To help both NASA and NAA, Boeing sent their third B-52A and fifth B-52B to NAA

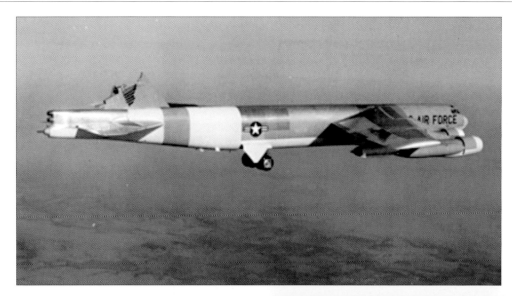

This B-52H was being used as a test bed to identify structural weaknesses in the airframe when its vertical stabilizer was sheared off. The crew, with the assistance of Boeing engineers on the ground, was able to land safely. (USAF)

for modification as launch aircraft for the X-15 programme, which had started at the end of 1954. The two aircraft were changed at the United States Air Force Plant 42, a classified aircraft manufacturing plant in the Mojave Desert, California. The B-52A was the first to arrive at Plant 42 at the end of November 1957; three months later, it was transferred to the NAA hangar. By the end of the year, the B-58B, later known as *Balls 8*, had arrived and was rapidly converted for use, arriving at NAA's hangar at the beginning of 1959.

The critical modification carried out was the addition of an underwing pylon on the starboard side inboard of the engine nacelles. This innocuous-looking addition could carry a staggering 50,000lbs (22,680kg) and assist in its carriage of the X-15. It was provided with shackles and the

NASA's NB-52B *Balls 8* showing off her mass of mission markings in 1993. (NASA/Dryden Flight Research Center)

Left: NB-52B *Balls 8* carries the experimental UAV Boeing X-43. (NASA/Tom Tschida)

necessary umbilical attachments to give the X-15 liquid oxygen, nitrogen, breathing oxygen, and electrical power. A 1,500-gal (6,819-l) liquid oxygen tank was installed in the bomb bay of each donor B-52. This was used to refill the X-15's tanks while carrying it to its optimum launch altitude of 45,000ft (13,716m). Another critical addition was fitting closed-circuit television and film motion picture cameras.

Five indicator lights were fitted on the fuselage starboard side to help coordinate the pilots' actions of the B-52 and X-15. Three of the lights confirmed that the pylon hooks were securely engaged. The 'ready to launch' light, which indicated all the necessary systems were ready for launch, and the launch light, which prepared the X-15 pilot for the launch countdown, was cockpit-operated. These visual cues were installed as a precaution after incidents earlier in the rocket programmes saw pilots inadvertently launching after an attempted abort. To initiate the launch of the X-15, a launch panel was installed on the upper deck of the B-52, where the operator could monitor the dangerous fuelling process and the other vital systems of the X-15. The launch panel allowed the altitude and velocity data to be fed directly into the X-15's inertial guidance computer until launch. The operator would eventually benefit from a Plexiglas dome on the upper deck of each of the NB-52s so they could make direct observations of the X-15. The release system for the X-15 was installed for operation by the pilot of the B-52.

To help compensate for the additional wing weight, and to reduce damage to the mothership, the number 3 main fuel tank, which had been located in the wing directly above the pylon, was removed. Further structural modifications included a notch being cut into the trailing edge of the starboard wing directly behind the X-15 pylon, made to accommodate the vertical stabilizer of the X-15. Other changes included disabling the inboard flaps and removing the rear gun turrets and wing-tip fuel tanks. Aside from the noticeable technical changes, the two NB-52s would initially be finished with fluorescent orange paint applied to the tail and nose surfaces. The wings and engine intakes were also given the orange fluorescent finish. This paint scheme was used widely on the aluminium-finished aircraft operating from Edwards AFB, as it allowed a downed aeroplane to be easily identified in the desert operating environment of the Mojave. Later, simple fluorescent orange bands were applied to the fuselage and wing only. On 15 October 1969, NB-52A was transferred to the 309th Aerospace Maintenance and Regeneration Center (AMARC) after seventy-two captive-carry and launches of X-15 series aircraft. It also captive-carried and launched Northrop's heavyweight lifting demonstrators, the M2-F2, HL10, and the Martin Marietta X-24 lifting body aircraft.

Balls 8 would carry out most of the X-15 captive-carry and launch flights, including the first launch of the X-15 in January 1960. It would eventually chalk up 159 captive-carry and launch missions for the X-15 programme, finishing in October 1968. Other captive-carry and launched missions included carrying the Martin Marietta X-24 lifting body aircraft; the

A close-up view of the Highly Maneuverable Aircraft Technology (HiMAT) research vehicle attached to a wing pylon on NASA's NB-52B during a 1980 test flight. (NASA)

Left: A close-up view of the X-38 research vehicle mounted under the wing of the NB-52B prior to a 1997 test flight. The X-38 was designed to help develop technology for an emergency crew return vehicle (CRV) for the International Space Station. (NASA/Tony Landis)

Below: NASA research pilot Bill Dana takes a moment to watch NASA's NB-52B cruise overhead after a research flight in the HL-10. (NASA)

remotely piloted Rockwell RPRV-870 HiMAT (Highly Manoeuvrable Aircraft Technology); and NASA's experimental X-43 uncrewed hypersonic aircraft. Other projects included carrying the Northrop series of Lifting Body aircraft and Orbital Sciences Corporation (OSC) Pegasus air-launched orbital launch vehicle.

At its retirement on 17 December 2004, *Balls 8* was the oldest active B-52 in service, and the only B-52 that was not an H model. It also had the lowest total airframe time of any operational B-52. Today, it can be seen keeping watch at the gates of its old home, Edwards Air Force Base, California.

RB-52B

The RB-52B could carry a pressurized, 300lbs (136kg), two-person reconnaissance pod. The pod, which took four hours to install, contained radio receivers and K-36, K-38, and T-11 cameras. The two operators were equipped with downward-firing ejection seats.

RB-52C

The RB-52C was initially given to B-52Cs similarly fitted for reconnaissance duties. As all thirty-five B-52Cs could be equipped with the reconnaissance pod, the RB-52C designation was of little use and was quickly abandoned.

JB-52B

In March 1956, JB-52B, known as *The Tender Trap*, became the first B-52 to leave the Continental United States as part of Operation Cherokee and headed to the Enewetak (Eniwetol) Atoll. There, along with other aircraft, including 52-0013, it monitored three effects of the tests: the post-explosion radiation levels, shock waves, and heat.

The X-15 is carried to its launch height by the NB-52B in this iconic photograph, showing how far powered aviation had come in fifty years. (NASA)

The colourful NB-52E
during the Air Force
Flight Dynamics
Laboratory-Boeing
Control Configured
Vehicles programme
(US Government)

TF-39 fitted onto the
JB-52E. (American
Aviation Historical
Society)

JB-52E

One aircraft leased by General Electric to test TF39 and CF6 engines.

NB-52E

The second production B-52E was designated to undertake major test programmes as part of the Air Force Flight Dynamics Laboratory-Boeing Control Configured Vehicles programme. Initially, it was used to test prototyping landing gears, engines, and other subsystems. As its role as a testbed developed, the B-52E received airframe and structural modifications to allow it to undertake specialized development projects and, as such, was redesignated NB-52E. The NB-52E was intended to study the effectiveness of electronic flutter and buffeting suppression systems. These had been designed as a result of the loss of several B-52s that had occurred due to structural failures caused by low-level flight-induced aerodynamic stresses. Small canards were attached below the cockpit, and a long probe was fixed to the nose. Another critical change included modifying the wings, which had their control surfaces doubled, and the traditional mechanical and hydraulic linkages that moved the control surfaces replaced by electronic systems. Accordingly, the interior of the

NB-52E was fitted with the necessary instrumentation to allow for accurate measurement of any testing carried out.

The NB-52E would later participate in the Load Alleviation and Mode Stabilization (LAMS) project. The project measured wind gusts through a battery of sensors that activated control surfaces to cut down on the amount of fatigue damage to the aircraft's structure. This system was so effective that in mid-1973, the NB-52E would fly 11mph (18km/h) faster than the speed at which flutter would have disintegrated the aircraft.

XR-16A

Allocated to the reconnaissance variant of the B-52B, but not used. The aircraft were designated RB-52Bs instead.

National Users

Regardless of being a well-known aeroplane, the B-52 was only used by the United States Air Force (USAF). In 2022, the USAF's B-52 force numbered seventy-two aeroplanes and these are currently operated by the following:

Air Combat Command
- 53d Wing – Eglin Air Force Base, Florida
  - 49th Test and Evaluation Squadron (Barksdale)

- 57th Wing – Nellis Air Force Base, Nevada
  - 340th Weapons Squadron (Barksdale)

- Air Force Global Strike Command
  - 2nd Bomb Wing – Barksdale Air Force Base, Louisiana
    - 11th Bomb Squadron
    - 20th Bomb Squadron
    - 96th Bomb Squadron
  - 5th Bomb Wing – Minot Air Force Base, North Dakota
    - 23d Bomb Squadron
    - 69th Bomb Squadron

The B-52H that replaced Dryden's NB-52B in December 2004. Sadly, it was returned to the USAF as no research projects requiring its capabilities emerged after NASA's restructured aeronautics research programmes. (NASA/Tony Landis)

- Air Force Materiel Command
  - 412th Test Wing – Edwards Air Force Base, California

- 419th Flight Test Squadron

- Air Force Reserve Command
  - 307th Bomb Wing – Barksdale Air Force Base, Louisiana
    - 93rd Bomb Squadron
    - 343rd Bomb Squadron

The National Aeronautics and Space Administration (NASA) has a long cooperation history with Boeing which continued with their use of the B-52 at their Dryden Flight Research Centre. Dryden is co-located at the USAF Edwards Air Force Base in California. NASA researches, develops, verifies, and transfers advanced aeronautics, space, and related technologies. Dryden is considered a Center of Excellence for atmospheric flight operations.

In 2001 NASA took delivery of a B-52H to replace the NB-52B which was due to retire in 2004. Delivery of the B-52H was initially as a loan, before transferring it from the USAF to NASA. The aircraft was intended to continue NASA's captive-carry and launched missions from Dryden Flight Research Centre at Edwards Air Force Base. To that end, NASA added a new carrier pylon, designed to adapt to various shapes and sizes, capable of carrying a 25,000lbs (11,340kg) load. This allowed the B-52H to act as a Heavy Lift Launch Aircraft, and the new pylon would let NASA perform design, analysis, and testing leading up to a Critical Design Review at the end of 2007. A flight research instrumentation package was installed following a complete de-militarization package and scheduled depot maintenance undertaken at Tinker Air Force Base, Oklahoma. This sat alongside other modifications which

NASA's new white NB-52H and veteran NB-52B were exhibited at Boeing Wichita, Kansas, on 12 April 2002, during the 50th anniversary of the B-52. (NASA/Tony Landis)

allowed the aircraft to fulfil its captive-carry and launch role. Sadly, with no research projects requiring its capabilities due to NASA's restructured aeronautics research programmes, the aircraft was returned to the USAF in May 2008. The plane was flown one last time to Sheppard Air Force Base, Texas, to become a GB-52H maintenance trainer.

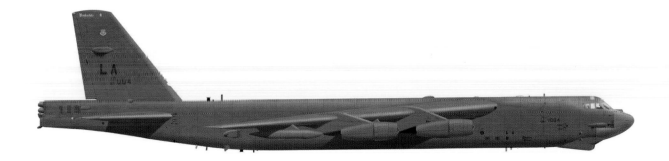

This B-52H belongs to 2nd Bombardment Wing, Barksdale AFB, Louisiana, as she appears in a series of US Pacific Command exercises that prepare joint forces to respond to crises in the region.

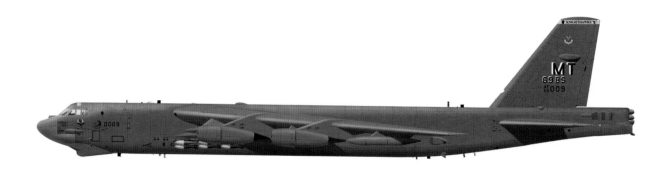

A B-52H from the 23rd Expeditionary Bomb Squadron, Minot AFB, North Dakota, operating from the Andersen Air Force Base, Guam during June 2013.

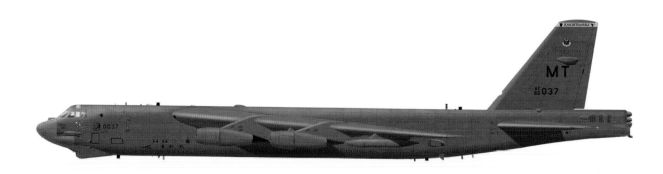

A B-52 from the 69th Expeditionary Bomb Squadron, Minot AFB, North Dakota, operating from the Andersen Air Force Base, Guam during July 2019.

A B-52H of the 11th Bomb Squadron/2nd Bomb Wing Barksdale AFB, Louisiana, as she appeared at the Royal International Air Tattoo, RAF Fairford, England, 2006.

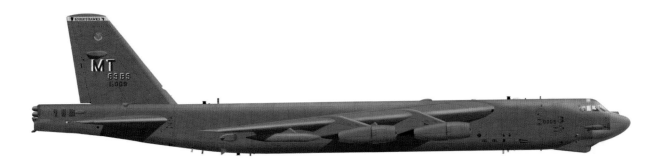

B-52H operating from Andersen Air Force Base, Guam, in August 2016, as one of the three Air Force Global Strike Command's strategic bomber aircraft that were conducting integrated operations in the US Pacific Command area of operations.

B-52D *Twilight D'Lite* currently on display at the Travis AFB Heritage Center, California. *Twilight D'Lite* last saw operational duty with the 7th Bomb Wing of the Strategic Air Command, Carswell AFB, Texas.

A NASA NB-52B *Balls 8* seen here with the experimental Unmanned Air Vehicle (UAV) Boeing X-43 unmanned hypersonic aircraft.

This B-52A is the oldest B-52 in existence; this is the third A model built and can be found at Pima Air and Space Museum, Arizona. It was also one of two B-52s modified to carry the North American X-15 rocket plane.

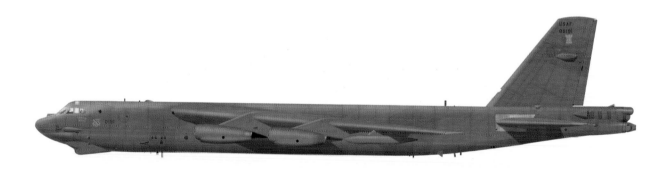

Two tone B-52G as it appeared at Air Force Materiel Command, Ogden, Hill AFB, Utah.

B-52D at South Dakota Air and Space Museum collection, Ellsworth Air Force Base, Rapid City, South Dakota.

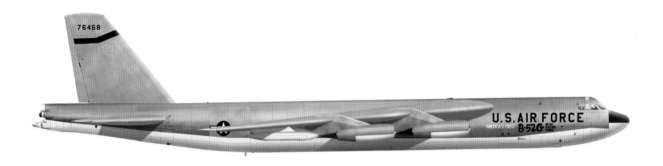

The first B-52G at its initial roll out on 28 July 1958 at Wichita, Texas, in silver and anti-flash white finish.

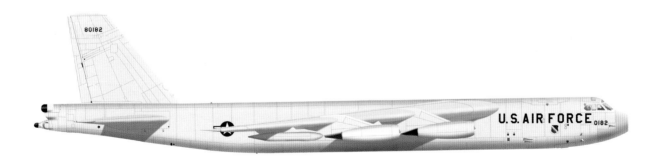

This B-52G from Edwards AFB, California, features an unusual all over white anti-flash finish that appears to have been restricted to this single aeroplane, perhaps as an experimental finish.

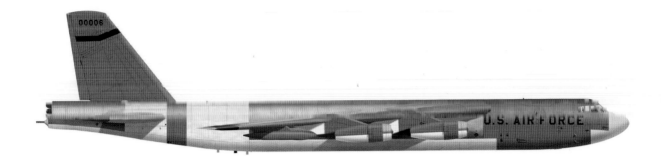

The NB-52B as seen at Edwards AFB, California, 1961. As the main exterior of this aircraft was unfinished metal, had it crashed, the surfaces would have reflected the surrounding desert, making location harder. The high-visibility paint was applied to overcome this and make locating lost aircraft easier.

B-52G, 43rd Strategic Wing which was based at Andersen AFB, Guam, as it appeared while taking part in Exercise Team Spirit, South Korea, 1985.

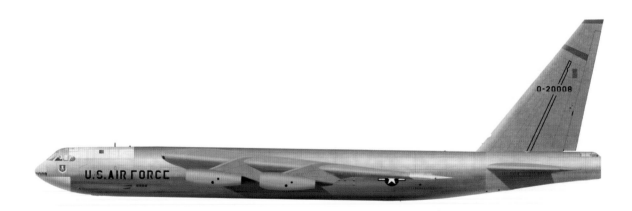

RB-52B in an early 1960s silver finish with white panels that eliminated glare, particularly over the top of the cockpit, to allow for safer mid-air refuelling. The RB-52B omitted any defensive armaments, and instead featured a curved glazed tail section.

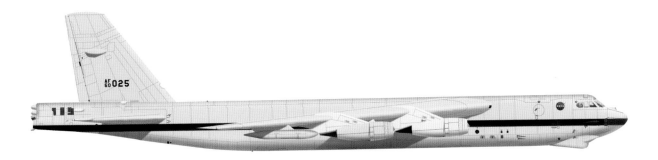

NASA obtained a B-52H bomber from the USAF in 2001 with the intention of using it as an air-launch and testbed platform to support NASA, Air Force and industry flight research and development. It was also scheduled to demonstrate advanced technology at NASA's Dryden Flight Research Center, Edwards AFB, California.

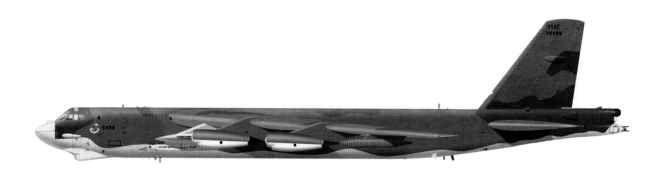

An air-to-air left side view of a B-52H Stratofortress aircraft as it flies over the Dugway Proving Grounds, Utah, Test and Training Range. Note the high visibility fuel tanks and the pylon-mounted AGM-86 ALCM.

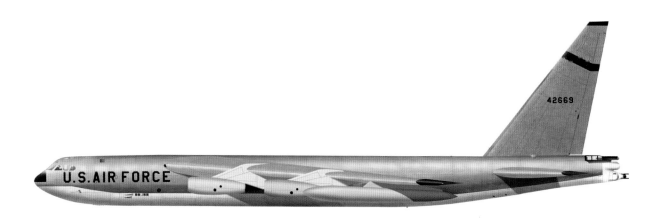

B-52C in its clean initial delivery finish. Of interest is the white anti-flash underside paint scheme that has been applied to the underside, but not over the cockpit.

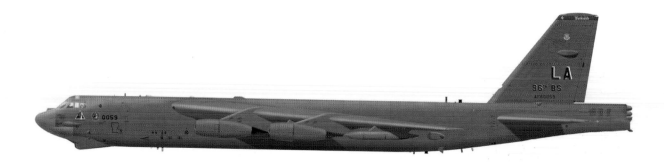

A rather weather-beaten Barksdale AFB, Louisiana, B-52H pictured on its deployment flight to RAF Fairford, June 2014.

A two-tone B-52G as it appeared in September 2015 at Barksdale Global Power Museum, Barksdale AFN near Bossier City, Louisiana.

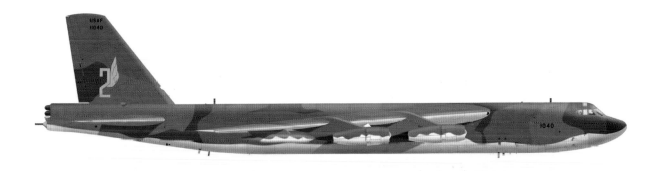

61-0040 was the last B-52H, and by extension the final B-52 ever built, rolling off Wichita's production line on 22 June 1962. It is seen here featuring a wonderful three-tone upper-surface camouflage pattern. Today this B-52 is in service with the 23rd Bomb Squadron, 5th Bomb Wing, at Minot AFB, North Dakota.

B-52H of 23rd Bomb Squadron, 5th Bomb Wing, at Minot AFB, North Dakota, November 2019.

B-52G, 28th Bomb Squadron,19th Bomb Wing, based at Robins AFB, Georgia, as it appeared during the Busy Brewer 82D exercise which ran between September and October 1982.

A two-tone B-52G as it appeared on an aerial mining mission off the South Korean coast during Exercise Team Spirit, held in 1986, designed to test US and South Korean defence plans and interoperability.

Modelling the Boeing B-52

The B-52 remains an extremely popular subject with modellers. It is well served by manufacturers who have produced a fantastic range of kits in all scales over the years. All kits have their merits, with great potential to add multi-media detailing and conversion parts, as well as changing markings; this helps the modeller create a personal build of this iconic aircraft. The available range of scales means the kits of such a large aeroplane can also be incorporated into vignettes in the smaller scales or impressive dioramas for those kits of 1/72 and 1/48. Such grand undertakings allow the modeller to experiment with other genres of model making, allowing them to introduce a range of ground-support vehicles and buildings. Unfortunately, new models of the B-52 are few and far between, mainly due to the subject's size, but detailing elements and decals continue to be produced. The following is purely contemporaneous, with featured manufacturers trading at the time of writing. For those wishing to build the more iconic vintage construction kits from Monogram, for example, there are often opportunities to purchase these from various sources.

Model Kits

Despite its size, the B-52 is well represented in 1/48, 1/72 and 1/144 scale model kits. These are available as vacuform and injection-moulded kits, with a more than admirable selection of after-market parts in various media to create something extra special. It is worth noting that some of the earlier kits, especially from Monogram's 1/72, have either been reboxed or been subject to corporate tie-ins by numerous companies, including AMT/ERTL, Bandai, Hasegawa, Revell, Italeri, and Modelcollect. Interestingly, Modelcollect has provided the modeller with a beautifully detailed kit, including the split-form forward fuselage section and detailed bomb bay, with their H-model kit featuring Conventional Rotary Launchers (CRL). All details are correct at the time of writing.

The BUFF's size is what makes it such a marvel for the larger-scale modellers, with Czech concern **HPH Models** producing a limited run of the H model (Nr. 48052L) in polyurethane resin, supplemented by photo-etch metal details as opposed to injection mould. Given the size of the finished model, this approach, allied with the use of internal bulkheads, gives the finished kit considerable strength. Utilizing cutting-edge CAD design, HPH has produced a multi-media kit that is as awe-inspiring as the real thing. The cockpit is awash with delicate detailing, while the faithfully replicated landing gear sets a benchmark that would be exceptionally hard to follow. That said, some parts are flimsy due to the exquisite detailing and the use of resin. Care is needed when building and working with resin, especially as some features must be sawn free of their casting blocks. As one would expect, the decals are plentiful and beautifully produced, and the colour instructions allow for a steady progression through the

B-52 STRATOFORTRESS 1/48 SCALE HpH models

B-52 H Stratofortress HpH 48052L 1/48 scale

B-52 STRATOFORTRESS 1/48 SCALE

assembly process; they also place the model firmly in the realms of the experienced modeller.

HPH Models have also produced a series of multi-media add-ons alongside this immense model. Nr. 48052-1 focuses on the MK.82 500lbs (136kg), Free Fall, General Purpose Bomb, providing pylon and bomb fittings and decals. Nr. 48052-2 features a Conventional Rotary Launcher (CRL), two pylons and twenty AGM-86 air-launched cruise missiles (ALCM), while Nr. 48052-3 presents the modeller with details for extended flaps. Interestingly, HPH Models have also produced a 1/32 kit of the forward fuselage crew areas for the H (Nr. 32044R), awash with details and hinting at a future larger-scale release of an already impressive kit.

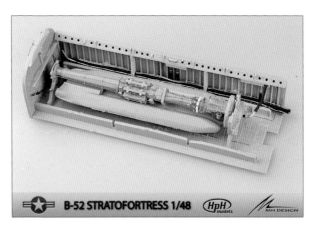

Welsh manufacturers **Sanger** produce multi-media, limited-run kits of all B-52 models from A to H, presenting the experienced modeller with a challenge that combines vacuformed styrene with photo-etch. As with all limited-run kits, this one requires considerable preparation and skill to build. The fuselage is broken down into four sections, as opposed to HPH's single section, with additional work needed to tidy the nacelles, especially the rear sections, which can be addressed by using a brass tube. The wings will require strengthening, remedial reworking of the flap areas, and the installation of a homemade spar. Sadly, the decals don't hold up to scrutiny, which can be challenging as third-party 1/48 decals are unavailable. However, it would be possible to home-produce or scavenge a set from other 1/48 kits.

As previously mentioned, the offering in 1/72 has been dominated by Monogram's 1968 kit (PA.215) of the D, which featured the novel addition of a battery-powered jet sound simulator. This kit remains in production as the G (Nr. 1451) and H (Nr. 1442) versions, produced by Italeri. External detailing is sharp, and a well-appointed upper-deck crew area is included; interestingly, the bomb bay is blanked off on this particular kit, but Italeri has provided underwing pylons for placing externally carried weapons systems. Wheel wells are well-designed and reasonably detailed, although there is more than enough scope for super detailing. A nice touch is the ease of adding the undercarriage after painting the overall airframe. Decals are sharp and plentiful, though consideration may be

given to painting the larger black wing and horizontal stabilizer lines. Both kits are beautifully presented, and although they feature a low-part count, they are excellent representations of the related B-52s. The instructions are clear, but the painting instructions, especially for the camouflaged mid- to late-Cold War versions, can be hard to make out. Considering the moulds' age, updated at some point, they feature a level of detail that one would expect with contemporary kits and give the modeller a satisfying build experience.

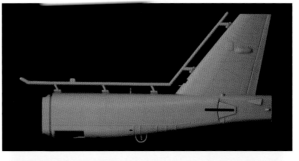

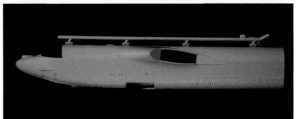

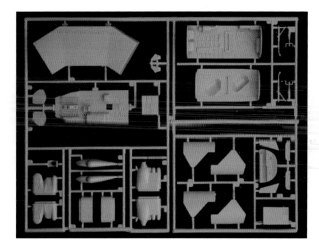
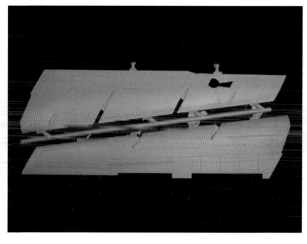

Chinese manufacturer **Modelcollect** offers the B-52 in the G (Nr. UA72212) and H models (Nr. UA72211) in 1/72, with many details needing to be included in the Italeri kits, including a complete cockpit and rear crew area and bomb bay. Both kits, including photo-etch, also feature the Conventional Rotary Launchers (CRL) and underwing mounted AGM-129s. Despite having an eight-piece fuselage for ease of construction, there are numerous minor issues with the finer details, including missing antennas, overly large wingtip fuel tanks and incorrectly shaped engine intakes on the H model. There are also challenges within the build process that require additional time to rectify, such as fixing AGM-86s to the CRL and needing bulkhead plates behind the landing gear. Initial kit instructions were deemed rather crude and have been updated. Cartograf has made the decals, though they appear dark grey instead of a more prototypical black. Modelcollect efforts give the modeller a decent base kit ripe for additional detailing.

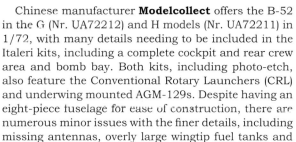

In 1/144, Academy, Great Wall, and **Minicraft** have all produced later model B-52s. Minicraft's offering (Nr. 14641) of the B-52H is the latest in a long line of Stratofortress-related kits available since 2012 in various guises. Their latest has a host of features from previous releases, including the GAM-87, AGM-28, and AGM-20, which can be used as stand-alone pieces. Interestingly, the traditionally split one-piece fuselage can be modified into an early G model and features the correct tail shape, proving Minicraft's attention to detail remains exceptional. To make the H model, Minicraft has supplied eleven extra pieces to add the necessary nose blisters and extend the tail. At this scale, the modeller is given a rudimentary cockpit. Also included are Cartograf decals that feature late 1980s colour national insignia and markings for the later gunship grey finished B-52s. Also present is a clear display stand for your completed build and individual stands for the missile. This allows the modeller to place the undercarriage in the raised position. For those seeking detailing options, Scale Aircraft Conversions has made a complete undercarriage replacement set in white metal (Nr.14414). Great Wall Hobby's late B-52G (Nr. L1009) and H (Nr. L1008) kits are remarkable for the sheer detail packed into these kits. For both kits, the internal detailing includes the lower deck to the forward fuselage, Conventional Rotary Launchers (CRL), one piece fuselage, and a range of stores, including the AGM-84, AGM-86C, MK.82 500lbs (136kg), and M117 750lbs (340Kg) demolition bomb. The kits are incredibly detailed, offering the modeller a range of finishing options, six for the G and two for the H. The instructions are well laid out, and the detailing of the parts and assemblies, at this scale, is remarkable. The G and H decals are colourful and appear correct for the versions covered. This is a challenging kit, but not demanding to the experienced modeller or the beginner with patience.

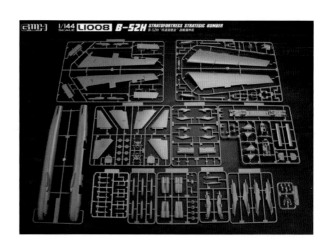

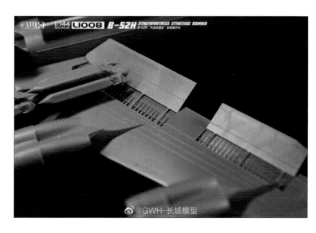

Academy offers the modeller the H (Nr.12622), which features Academy's almost legendary ease of construction and attention to detail. The kit features a full bomb bay, remarkable details such as moulded underbelly antennas, undercarriage options, and wonderfully detailed engines. Unlike Great Wall Hobby, Academy has settled to provide the modeller with the upper cockpit only, enclosed by a beautifully refined and well-engineered traditionally split one-piece fuselage. Unlike the other 1/144 kits, Academy has not held back with their decals, including the 'No Step' markings. The kit features cockpit masks and options to build three differing versions of the H, all in Gunship Grey.

The final kit of the fine-scale offerings is the **Atlantis** 1/175 B-52 with X-15, a remarkable kit almost as old as the B-52. This noteworthy kit, first released in 1954 by Revell, continues to sell, if only for its nostalgia value. While nowhere near as detailed as its 1/144 contemporaries, Atlantis delivers a straightforward and pleasurable build, which can be finished in either basic USAF or NASA finishes. The model lacks any cockpit detail, undercarriage, or armament. It is mounted on a transparent base, with the X-15 hanging from its pylon in the correct position under the starboard wing.

Regarding accuracy and detail, this kit is understandably at the back of the pile. Still, its vintage and easy assembly are a modeller's joy. Its size allows the new modeller to grapple with something different and allows the experienced modeller to have fun.

For those wanting to add extra detail, there are a few additional kits available. For those wanting a maritime slant on their B-52 build, Ukrainian company ResKit has produced an absolute arsenal of finely 3D-printed stores with photo-etch and decal details. These kits cover the AGM-84, GBU-54, and M117 bombs in 1/72, 1/48, and 1/32 scales.Czech photo-etch legends Eduard offers the Modelcollect G and H builder their

beautifully finished coloured internal detail sets Nr. 73646 (G) and Nr. SS657 (H) and a mask sheet for the G (Nr.CX531) shows they remain in touch with modelling's ever-changing trends.

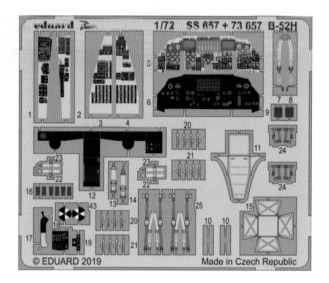

UK concern Aircraft in Miniature has built up a loyal following with its eclectic selection of kits. For those wanting to produce a 1/72 ground engineering scene or dispersal dioramas, they have produced a series of cast metal kits, including a B-52 Big Belly munitions trolley with the relevant bomb clips.

Also available in 1/72 are US firm Click2Details 3D printed conversion kits and detailing elements. Their XB-52 tandem seat-conversation kit is available in 1/144 and 1/72, including a revised tail cone, forward fuselage, wheelsets, cockpit, and clear canopy. It is worth noting that some work is required to remove the print lines. Also included in the range are B-52H TF33 engine sets in 1/72 and 1/48 and GAM-87 missiles and pylons. **Black Dog** Resin from the Czech Republic offers

the modeller two of their Big Set resin collections for the adventurous and experienced B-52 modeller wanting that little more. The first, Nr. A72020, features a detailed bomb bay and nose-mounted avionics bay, the second, Nr. 72017, features a beautifully designed and detailed Pratt & Whitney J57-P-43WB. Also featured in this set are the sizable extended wing flaps, supplemented with detailed wing sections. All kits are tailored for Italeri's G model and are available as single items.

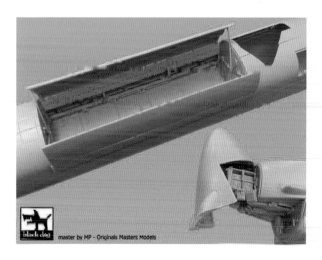

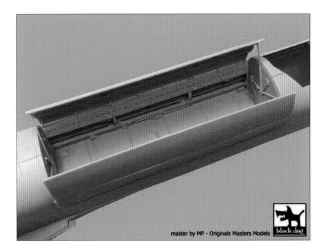
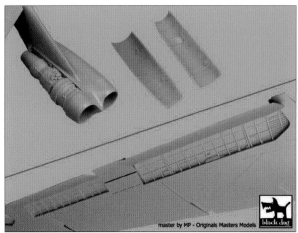
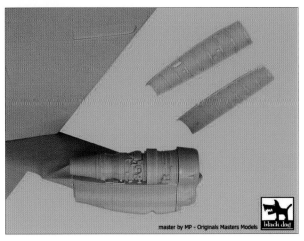
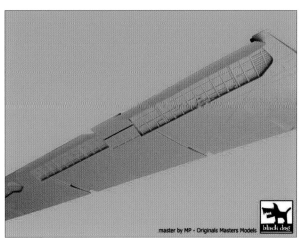

US firm **Contrails** provides two resin kits for 1/144 B-52s. The first set covers the NB-52 A/B *Balls 8*, while the second provides all the elements needed for a D model conversion. Both include replacement tails, forward fuselage, engine pods, tails and, in the case of the D conversion, rear-gunner position and gun set.

Today, for most modellers, one of the most important accessories is the transparency masks. These have been produced for 1/72 and 1/144 scales by various companies, including KV Models (No. 72098), Kit Mask (No. 72-014), New Ware (No. NWAM0902), and Aolt (No. 000 M14401). The final details for any build will always be the decals. Not surprisingly, there are plenty to choose from, with the Warbird (No. 72021)

set covering six G and H models, including the NASA B-52H. Interestingly, they've gone for those B-52s with the most colourful nose art, and the illustrations are beautifully reproduced. Almark Decals has produced an exciting collection covering the A, NB-52A, NB-52E, and the G that capture the spirit of the early colourful SAC markings often found on B-52s in the early 1950s. German manufacturer Herpa produced a single set of decals for the G (No. 572767) during Operation Secret Squirrel in the Operation Desert Shield stages of the 1991 Gulf War. The colourful nose art, in particular, is beautifully captured and well defined, with all colours in register, giving the modeller an excellent opportunity to create a unique and important B-52.

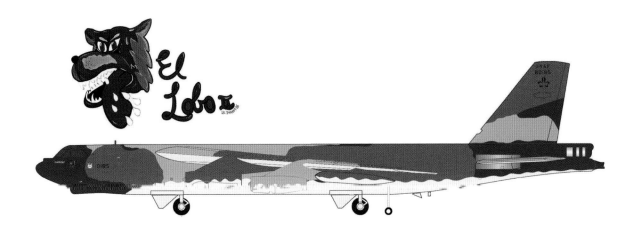

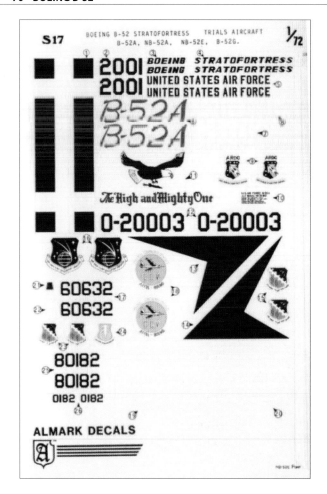

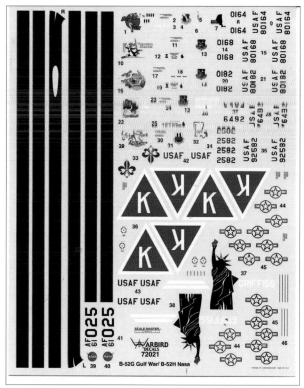

Left: Almark decals.
Above: Warbird decals.
Below left and right: caracal Models' decals.
Page 71 bottom: Herpa livery.

For the 1/144 modeller, **Caracal Models** have produced a series of decals for the later G and H models, offering the modeller a choice from no fewer than eleven finishes. Given the size of the 1/144 B-52, which averages at 340 x 390 x 130mm, there is a real opportunity to create a wing of uniquely finished B-52s.

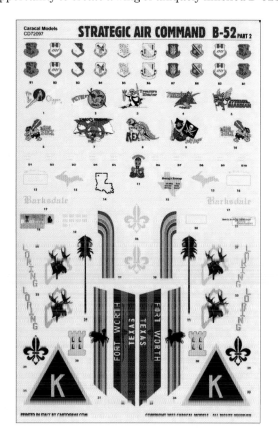

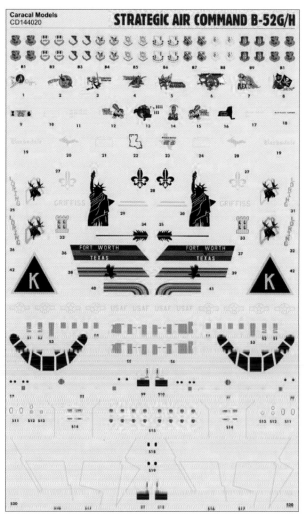

**Dragon 1/200th
NB-52B w/X-15A-2 & Pegasus
Andrew Newstead**

This is a model I built a long time ago as part of a project for 1/200th-scale crewed US spacecraft. It was made to be displayed alongside the AMT 'Man in Space' set and the Hasegawa Space Shuttle, showing all the crewed spacecraft flown by the United States up to that time. The model consisted of a Boeing B-52 in 1/200th scale with an accompanying North American X-15 A-2 rocket plane and the Grumman Pegasus satellite launcher rocket, carried aloft by the B-52 for launching. The B-52 was a popular subject with Dragon in the 1990s. They produced many of the different bomber variants using the same basic kit with different parts' frames to ring the many changes to the aircraft. This one is the B-52B, featuring the tall tail fin, rounded, smooth nose and earlier engines. The kit also contained extra parts for the test-aircraft variant of the model.

NASA used two of these aircraft at Edwards AFB for research purposes by carrying aloft experimental aircraft prototypes to be released at altitude, particularly notable is the X-15 rocket plane. This craft was designed to fly at hypersonic speeds (greater than Mach 5) and extreme altitudes over 50 miles high. It was a small reusable spacecraft, and its pilots would earn astronaut status when flying it at this height.

The kit was relatively straightforward to build. Some adjustments needed to be made to the basic kit parts to allow for the appropriate variant parts to be fitted; some cuts were required to remove material, and holes needed filling where some features were not used. Some filling was required at the wing roots. The model included a unique mounting pylon under the port wing to carry the X-15 and the later Pegasus rocket. For the display, I didn't wanted the X-15 to be mounted on the B-52 but to stand alongside the B-52 mother ship, so I scratch-built a representation of the rocket plane's undercarriage to allow it to stand alongside the B-52.

One of the distinctive features of the early B-52B was that it needed a natural aluminium metal finish, for which I used a spray can of Humbrol's Aluminium Metalcote paint. This is a buffable paint applied to a surface and then buffed to a metallic finish. I wanted a slightly oxidized look to the metal, so I buffed it lightly and then used a satin varnish spray to seal the painted surface. Some panel detail was picked out with a simple black paint wash.

Italeri B - 52G 1/72
B-52G *El –Lobo*
Paulo Fonseca,

On 16 January 1991 seven B-52s of the 596th Bomb Squadron, 2nd Bomb Wing, left Barksdale AFB, Louisiana, in the early hours of the morning to undertake one of the longest combat missions in history. It was known as Operation Senior Surprise/Secret Squirrel. The aim of this thirty-five-hour return flight of 14,000mi (22,531km), supported by four mid-air refuellings, was to destroy Iraqi command-and-control assets with GPS-guided AMG-86C Conventional Air Launched Cruise Missiles (CALCM), the first time these weapons had been used in combat.

This B-52G features one of the B-52s that took part, *El –Lobo*, and uses various detailing elements, including the Black Dog resin kits No. 72017 and No. A72020 and Herpa decals No. 572767 to create an outstanding build of Italeri's B-52G No. 1378. The build follows the instructions, with the crew positions in the forward fuselage strengthened and kept in place by strips of sprue. It was further secured to the lower nose with ticker sections of sprue and epoxy resin. The rear fuselage section is secured with epoxy resin, sprue, and a short collar to ensure a stable fixing to the forward fuselage section. The wing spar box was also strengthened with vertical and horizontal sprues. The wings were changed to show them in their drooped or grounded aspect, as the kit supplies them in their flying profile. The Black Dog resin parts were cleaned, the moulded kit wing flaps were removed, and the

Black Dog replacement sections were added, with styrene strips used to provide bulkheads.

For finishing, all parts were primed using AK758 grey primer and microfiller before they were pre-shaded black, with the cockpit areas completed in AK RC251 dark ghost grey and the wheel bays and internal wing areas finished in chromium yellow. The Pratt and Whitney J-75 resin engine was finished using enamel and acrylic paints.

After final assembly, the entire model was primed and pre-shaded with the three-colour paint scheme masked and applied in stages on the upper surfaces, with a light grey underside. The model was then varnished, with decals applied and sealed before a black wash was applied to bring out recessed panels and details. Overall, it was an enjoyable build experience, with the completed model forming the centrepiece of a larger diorama.

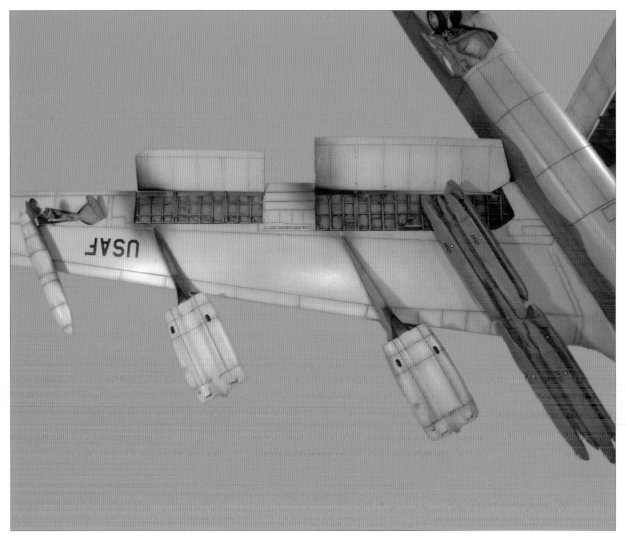

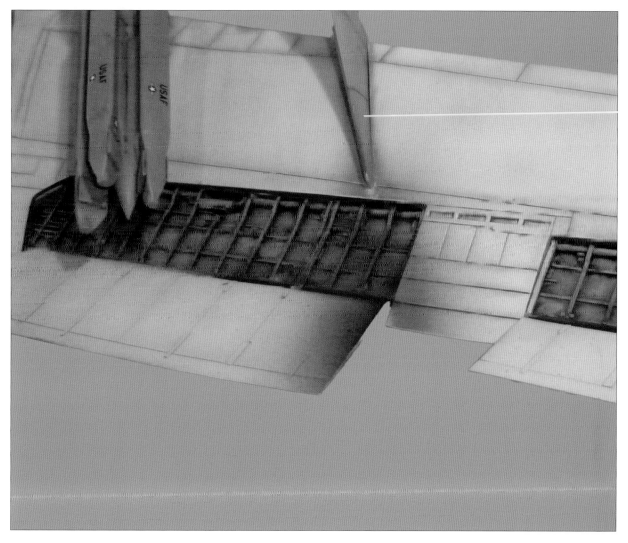

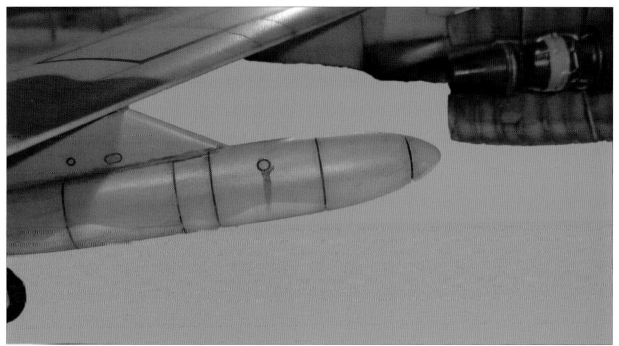

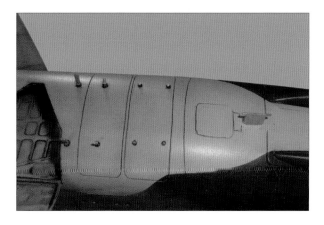

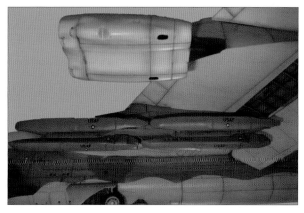

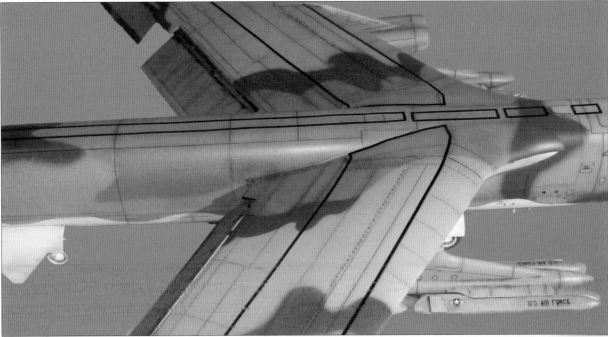

Italeri B-52G-90-BW Stratofortress 1/72
Mohawk Warrior (S/N 57-6515)
801st BW, Moron AB, Spain, February 1991

This Italeri re-boxing (1378) of the AMT/ERTL kit was released in 2016 for the 25th anniversary of the Gulf War. From the start the box art is a bit misleading as it shows a straight wing root when in fact the kit is the version fitted with the wing root fairing. This was added to aircraft of the nuclear deterrent force that carried air-launched cruise missiles (ALCMs). At the time this was a condition of the SALT II treaty.

This limits the modeller to only two versions from the four supplied on the kit decal sheet, that is 'Let's Make a Deal' pictured on the box or 'Mohawk Warrior', which was the one chosen for this build. Italeri has also re-boxed two other Gs and a choice of two different H kits.

This aging kit does have its issues and I was able to correct most of them. The main problem areas that require quite bit of surgery are the lack of wing droop for a model on the ground and the tail section taper needs extensive filling with card, putty, and a lot of sanding. It's too narrow by about 6mm.

Black Dog has provided a few resin upgrades for those wishing to enhance their builds further and I used their wing flap set as all B-52s on the ground have their flaps down except those undergoing maintenance. Armory Models' weighted wheels are a big improvement and replaced the kit parts.

Here's a list of other work starting from the nose and moving toward the rear:

- The bulge each side below the cockpit was reshaped and the two 'lumps' below that were removed and drilled to take pitot tubes which were added later.
- Various air intakes were opened up and blanked off with card.

- Ripple skin effect was created with a mini rotary tool fitted with a round burr and feathered in with Mr Surfacer and a lot of sanding.
- Before closing up the fuselage the kit's wing box, part 36K, was modified and strengthened to allow the wings to droop.
- Rear fuselage butt straps need sanding down and some riveting detail was added with a roller tool.
- Many panel lines were filled and re-scribed as they're too heavy for this scale.
- The horizontal stabilizer pivot plates need a couple of recesses filled in and reshaped as they shouldn't be there. Stabilizers also need to be re-worked to get a good fit.
- The vertical stabilizer was re-attached after the tail taper was corrected. This was reinforced with some styrene rod to strengthen the joint.
- The tail also received some raised panels and some detailing with four brass .50cal gun barrels from Master Models were added at the end of the build. These were left over from a B-17 job, and as I was sure to knock these off if they were added too soon, they were left until the very last.
- The kit doesn't provide any guns, only the tail barbet with four empty holes.
- The wing flaps were removed from the lower half with Black Dog replacements added.
- Out rigger wheel wells also had some ribs added with styrene as these are completely devoid of any detail.
- Tamiya XF4 Lemon Yellow is a close match for the chromate and a Tamiya black panel line wash weathered this in nicely.
- Starting on the engine nacelles, air intake vents were opened by drilling and were finished with a file, and new intake bullets replaced the undersized kit parts.
- Exhaust nozzles were added from tube.

Modelling the Boeing B-52 **87**

Work then progressed to the Conventional Air-Launched Cruise Missiles (CALCMs) and these received folded wings and pitot's made from 0.4mm copper wire. Each CALCM also received an exhaust cover punched from card and painted black during the final stages.

Moving to the undercarriage, the legs were detailed with copper wire brake lines and a few bolt heads and raised pins on all hinge joints. The kit wheels were also replaced with Armory Models' wheels. These need drilling out for different kits. I also decided to drill the undercarriage legs and replace the axle pins with metal rod for more strength. This model was already getting heavy, and it wasn't even finished, the last thing I needed was for a wheel to snap off. Undercarriage doors had some riveting done and a

locking latch added. I've omitted to add landing lights as that section of the door isn't quite the right shape to take them.

It is noteworthy how much filling with card and putty is required at the wing roots and pylons. All the little lumps and bumps, sensors and so on were added into pre-drilled holes after painting and decals. This saved a lot of re-work having to re-attach.

Mr Color 305 Gray FS36118 USAF was the main colour chosen and this was adjusted with SMS white and some of their grey colours to add a little variation to an otherwise rather bland scheme. Kit decals work very well but do require careful handling, especially the wing walk lines. These are quite long, and I cut some of them into sections for an easier fit.

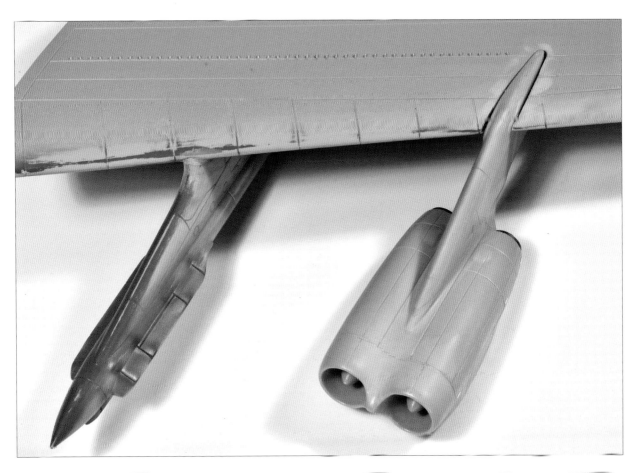

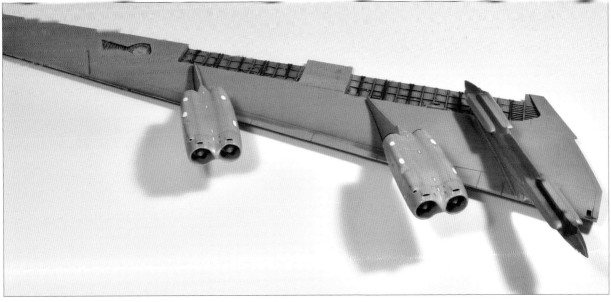

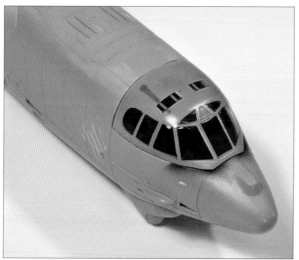

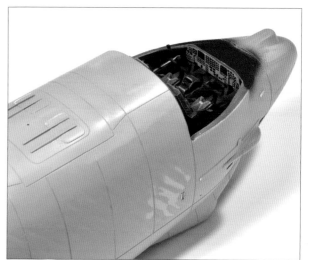

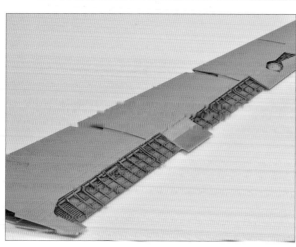

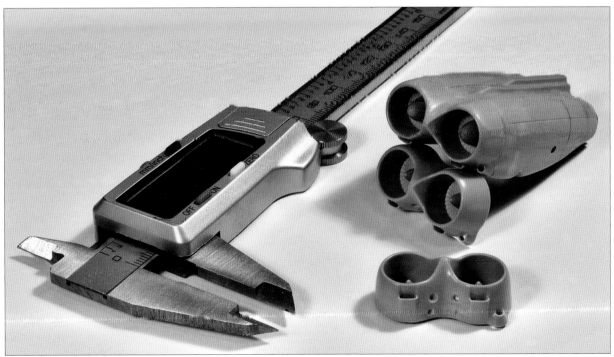